International Lathe-Turned Objects

DEDICATION

To all the people who entered *Challenge IV*,
whether they were selected or not . . .

TOUR SCHEDULE:

PORT OF HISTORY MUSEUM
Philadelphia, Pennsylvania
May 17 through August 4, 1991

UNIVERSITY ART MUSEUM
Arizona State University
Tempe, Arizona
September 8 through November 3, 1991

NORTHERN ARIZONA UNIVERSITY
Art Museum and Galleries
Flagstaff, Arizona
November 20, 1991 through January 1, 1992

CRAFT & FOLK ART MUSEUM
Los Angeles, California
February 1 through April 12, 1992

Published on the occasion of the opening venue of *International Lathe-Turned Objects: Challenge IV*, Port of History Museum, Philadelphia, Pennsylvania, May 17 through August 4, 1991.

The exhibit was co-sponsored by the Wood Turning Center, Philadelphia, and the Port of History Museum, City of Philadelphia.

CREDITS

PHOTO CREDITS

All photos provided by artists or by the following:

Dennis and Iona Elliott, *Aviary Abode* and *Portrait of Wren Cottage* by A. Barnum

Tom Griffin, *Plate Form #15001* by B. Behrens

David Haas, *Mother/Daughter: Hunter/Prey II* and *Frog Bowl II* by M. Brolly

Joy Fox, earlier work by P. Brown

Robert Jaffe, *Tomb Of An Unknown King* by C. Burchard

Christopher Briscoe, earlier work by C. Burchard

Tommy Elder, *Untitled* by R. W. Chatelain

Isabelle Lacey, *Thistle Head Pot* by P. Clare

Michel Focard de Fontefiguiéres, earlier work by P. Clare

Art Rogers Photography, earlier work by A. Clarke

Mark Fainstein, *Walking Stool* by N. Donovan

Al Abrams, *Memory Of The Sea*, *Dunes Series #5*, *Calligraphy* and earlier work by V. Dotson

Harold Wood, *Redemption* and earlier work by C. Forster

John Carlano, *Relationships II*, *The Insight* by G. Gilson

Tony Boyd, earlier work by S. Hogbin

D. Hard, earlier work by M. Holzapfel

Bobby Hanson, earlier work by D. Kelly

Chris Bartol Photography, *Metropolis #3* and *Resonance* by S. Lamar

Eric Mitchell, earlier work by W. Leete

Tony Geraldi, *Memories of East Texas* by S. Loar

Stephen M. Spinder, *Untitled* (both) and earlier work by A. Macdonald

Francois Melilo, *Translucent Goblets* by A. Martel

Harold Wood, *Tea Balance* and earlier work by W. Moore

Rich Killion Photography, *Human Nature*, *Viper* and earlier work by D. Mueller

Rickey Yanaura, earlier work by C. Nutt

Eric Mitchell, earlier work by S. Paulsen

Roger Schreiber, earlier work by M. Peterson

Richard Sargent, *Spiral Stairs to Zaccahaeus*, *Red Square X Four* and *Captive Pink* by J. Sauer

Hermann Wehmeyer, *Ball-Box, Turned Broken Through* by H. J. Weissflog

Kramer's Photography, *Curious* by D. Wentz

Ted Wolff, *Pomegranate Time* (both) and earlier work by L. Wolff

COVER:

Sculptured die (Sterling Embossing) from photo of *Curious* by David Wentz.

EDITORS

EILEEN J. SILVER
MARY R. HEYING
TINA C. LeCOFF

DESIGN AND PRODUCTION

AEGIS PRODUCTIONS, INC.:
EILEEN J. SILVER
KAY GERING
STEVE PARKER
MARY R. HEYING

LINOTRONIC IMAGING

PCI GROUP

PRINTER

LARRY NEIBAUER,
NEIBAUER PRESS

Library of Congress Catalog Card Number: 91-06578
ISBN: 0-9624385-3-7

Printed in the United States of America

CONTENTS

Sponsors' and Jurors' Statements

Sponsors

Ronald Barber, Director
Port of History Museum
Philadelphia, Pennsylvania, United States

The Port of History Museum is pleased to host the *International Lathe-Turned Objects: Challenge IV* exhibition. This exhibit reflects the continued commitment by the Port of History Museum to work with the various cultural and art organizations of Philadelphia to produce unique exhibitions. The work selected for this show falls into a variety of categories, however the aspect of challenge was a primary focus in the choosing of the lathe-turned objects. It is with continued pleasure and distinction that the Port of History Museum and the Wood Turning Center have joined together in presenting this exhibit.

Albert B. LeCoff, Executive Director
Wood Turning Center
Philadelphia, Pennsylvania, United States

In 1987, the **Craft Alliance** in St. Louis asked me to curate a show of lathe-turned objects. I believed that anyone could put together a quality exhibition with a group of known artists. What I wanted to do was to further the *collective* growth of the lathe-turning field by challenging promising, emerging artists, as well as established artists to submit one new piece reflecting their search for self expression. In response, I curated a show called *Works Off The Lathe: Old and New Faces*. One of the main goals was to bring out the high quality and diversity of lathe-turned work. There were as many types of lathes, techniques, and objects as there were people using the lathe. The materials ranged from natural to man-made, including wood, metal, ivory, stone, precious gems, and plastics.

The *Challenge* exhibitions I curated the next two years, 1988 and 1989, included fifty to sixty artists whose work represented unique aspects of lathe-turning. In them, I sensed an energy that sparked new directions that would expand the profile of the lathe-turning field. Challenging the artists gave them an opportunity to expand, but collectors and the public were also challenged when they saw the exhibits, for they were forced to confront their preconsceptions about function, decoration, and sculpture. In addition, each exhibition included a conference entitled *The Purpose of the Object: Why We Create, Why We Collect*. This created a dialogue between artists and collectors.

The 1991 *Challenge* took on a new name—**International Lathe-Turned Objects: Challenge IV**— and was organized by the **Wood Turning Center**. *Challenge IV* represents a change from invited shows to a completely juried show. This allowed both established and emerging artists to present work for consideration by specialists from the craft/art world. The jurors represented diverse professional views. They included museum curator Ned Cooke, sculptor Stephen Hogbin, and ceramist/educator Rudolf Staffel. Artists were asked to submit color slides, personal statements, and photos of previous work as a reference point. All of the works were juried. After review of all of the submitted materials, the jurors selected a diverse group of work that reflected significant lathe-created art.

I am grateful to all of the entrants because they force the field to expand, whether they were selected or not. The work submitted showed the artists' continued movement from materials and techniques, to design and self expression. In many ways, it was painful to turn the selection over to jurors, and I am sure that in some ways the process was painful for artists. I venture to say, though, that there is always some pain in growth. This process forced me to stop, look, and listen.

What we get out of *Challenge IV* is a diverse sample of current work, organized into themes by the jurors after selection. The catalog and exhibition are organized to reflect the field of lathe-turning, not a field of individuals. The things that stand out in my mind are the nature of the work created during a recession and during a War in the Middle East, and the fact that so many expressive objects were created using the same basic technical process, lathe-turning.

Jurors

Edward S. Cooke, Jr., Associate Curator
American Decorative Arts and Sculpture
Museum of Fine Arts
Boston, Massachusetts, United States

Embracing Plurality

For scholars of the visual arts who seek to recognize pattern and direction, plurality of expression often elicits negative responses. Diffuse, unrelated work of a particular period or artist is sometimes viewed skeptically, as a symptom of incoherent drift or of not-yet-resolved ideas. Yet plurality of style or expression does not necessarily mean that there are no shared values or bonds.

After jurying *Challenge IV* I realized that the field of turning has really matured beyond its earlier focus upon pure form and beautiful grain. Just ten years ago, other manipulation and decoration was considered inappropriate since it obscured the form or the grain. Work from 1991 demonstrates incredible diversity: continued refinement of restained formal purity; incorporation of burls, heartwood, sapwood, and bark; use of paint and artificial materials; and development of narrative or political statements. All of this expressive pluralism is linked, however, by a solid base in the use of the lathe. It is this foundation in a specific process that links the infinite choices included in this stunning exhibition. While the individual works are compelling in their own right, they resonate more powerfully as a whole.

Albert LeCoff's courage and vision to once again challenge all of the members of the turning field has paid off. The works we chose for the exhibition all demonstrate that intent and performance continue to reach new heights. Emphasis on ideas, forms, or techniques can be integrated within the field of lathe-turned objects. The resulting objects, materials, and treatments are varied but all are connected by the lathe. This link provides parameters for comparison, evaluation, and ultimately understanding.

STEPHEN HOGBIN, SCULPTOR
OWEN SOUND, ONTARIO, CANADA

Like the blank sheet of paper on which a mark is placed, the turning blank has become the surface for new marks. But as origami is about the physicality of paper, so too does turning have its physical aspects. Understanding and appreciating the material, and how to work it on the lathe, should remain central to the activity, while the imagination explores the form of our relationship with the chaos, complexity, and conformity of the world that surrounds us.

The blank sheet of paper has never finally deterred the creative mind from finding ways to resolve feelings, express ideas, communicate knowledge, and find some delight in the agony of the process. Turning is the blank sheet in which a community of people develop insight. It is an activity that seems endlessly capable of developing skill and knowledge but, most importantly, it sustains the imagination. The jury on this occasion was concerned primarily with the imagination and aesthetic challenge rather than the skill or knowledge challenge. But, clearly some exceptional skill and knowledge was the foundation for an aesthetic quality.

I have not been as deeply involved with turning as I used to be. My interests have shifted in part from the turning activity. It was then with considerable interest that I watched the 1100 slides of 122 people's work and struggled with the selection of an excellent group of work. There were some extremely tough choices to make. Tough because the quality of work was high.

The jury consistently reflected on the idea of the challenge. The written statements were far more varied in quality than the objects, but we were not jurying statements. However they certainly helped direct us to how the makers reflected on their work and the personal challenge they were meeting.

The challenge for most of the participants in this event did not seem to be caught up in *sharp looking images,* using an excess of materials, that would reproduce well in colorful magazines. The submissions were not objectified into media objects that look merely clever, expensive, and consumptive. Most of the work, by and large, was directed and went beyond the tyranny of the blank sheet of paper, the wonder of flying ribbons of wood chips or the mystery of growth patterns in wood, to express ideas which were clearly felt and thought out.

We carefully selected useful and beautiful objects that are from the craft tradition. We searched for the content of the maker's experience to see where the activity of turning had contextually connected their skill and knowledge imaginatively with their lives. This had taken place in various overlapping and intersecting ways and the catalog offers a coarse/course categorization that may help suggest some broad ways of thinking about the maker's intention—inevitably some works could have existed in more than one category.

At this point the objects in *Challenge IV* show an interest in contextual work but, the full range of bioregional, biocratic, omnicentral, and being in place has yet to be fully explored and realized. However, it seems the purpose of the object reveals to a large degree the subject of our lives in context through the evolving spin of a blank turning.

RUDOLF STAFFEL, CERAMIC ARTIST,
PROFESSOR EMERITUS,
TYLER SCHOOL OF ART
PHILADELPHIA, PENNSYLVANIA, UNITED STATES

My recent experience of being one of the jurors of the recent lathe-turned objects exhibition has been a rewarding revelation to me. Rewarding and revelatory because it once again reveals the power of the creative surge of the human spirit.

What amazing excitements and inventive surprises can be accomplished in the use of the hand, the tool and the material when confronted by a challenge—the challenge of using a noble and utilitarian skill brought to a level of evocative artistic excitement. This is the *way* of crafts and why wood turning is a well-respected art, and has an ever-growing audience.

As a teacher of crafts these last 50 years, I have had the privilege of participating and witnessing this transformation many times—in clay, in glass, in fibres and wood. It is high time wood turning and lathe work took its rightful place in the teaching activities of the art schools.

ACKNOWLEDGMENTS

The exhibition, production of this catalog, and the tour, were made possible through the generosity of the following individuals and organizations:

BENEFACTORS
Ruth Greenberg
Don Roy King
Kiss Fresh Fruit, Co.
Pennsylvania Council on the Arts
Howard Peters
Shopsmith, Philadelphia, PA
Barry S. Slosberg, Inc.

SPONSORS
Irv Lipton
Arthur and Jane Mason
Nordy Rockler, The Woodworkers' Store

PATRONS
Connell Gallery/Great American Gallery
del Mano Gallery
Gallery Fair
Edward "Bud" Jacobson
Charles and Doro Kerr
Mendelson Gallery
Northwest Gallery of Fine Woodworking
Sansar Gallery
Seldom Seen Gallery
Snyderman Gallery

SUPPORTERS
Sandra Blain
Delta International Machinery
C.R. "Skip" Johnson
Ed Moulthrop
Stan Pence
Ruth and David Waterbury

LENDERS OF OBJECTS

Peter Joseph Gallery, *Time Piece* by Michelle Holzapfel

Irv Lipton, *Mother/Daughter: Hunter/Prey II* by Michael Brolly; *Textured Jar* by John Jordan; *Fossil I Series* by Michael Peterson; and *Civilization As They Knew It #5, Catacombs & Fusion Chamber* by Stephen Paulsen

Rude Osolnik, *Memories of East Texas* by Stephen Loar

Snyderman Gallery, *Silver Maple Bowl* by Phil Brown

SPECIAL THANKS TO...

the members of the Wood Turning Center for their continued financial support…

the board of the Wood Turning Center for their guidance and support…

the Port of History Museum: Ron Barber, director; and his excellent staff: Corliss F. Cavalieri, curator of exhibits and Zenon L. Feszczak, design director…

Eileen, Eileen, Eileen Silver!

Alan LeCoff, my brother, for his continued and unconditional assistance and advice…

Tina LeCoff, my wife, for her assistance in writing and editing the catalog and her willingness to put up with my endless hours on the phone and at the computer.

—ALBERT B. LECOFF, COORDINATING CURATOR

EXHIBITION CATALOG

The following pages show all of the selected works in the exhibition, *International Lathe-Turned Objects: Challenge IV.*

Presented with each piece, when possible, is a photo of the artist's earlier work and their personal statement.

The following abbreviations are used in giving the dimensions of each piece:

    height: H.

    width: W.

    depth: D.

  diameter: Diam.

PART ONE

MATERIAL AND PROCESS

CHAPTER ONE

THE CLASSIC FORM

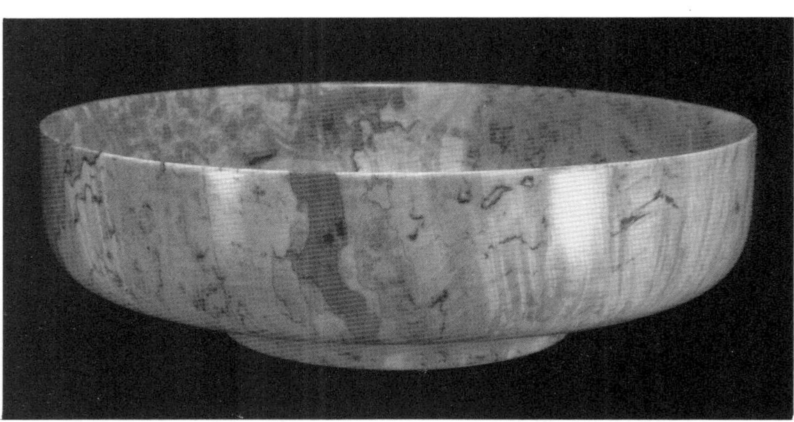

Silver Maple Bowl. Silver maple. H. 3 1/8" x Diam. 10"

This challenge was to achieve a fruit bowl appearing and being light in weight from a nicely figured burly silver maple flinch which varied in firmness from hard to quite soft, reflecting different progressions of decay. Alternate turning, firming with clear epoxy paint, turning, treating again and sanding have proved to be a successful progression in achieving my desired result. This piece is inspired by, and in homage to, Bob Stocksdale.

PHIL F. BROWN
MARYLAND, UNITED STATES

Boxelder Burl Bowl. Boxelder burl.
H. 6 5/8" x Diam. 7 5/8 "

The challenge of this bowl was to create a new piece that satisfied my wish for expression. For the last few years, my prime purpose has been to create bowls that resonate with my own needs. This bowl fulfills such a need. Besides being a visually pleasing and sensuous object, it serves as a tangible symbol of the mystery of the creative process. To me, a bowl is successful if it is an honest reflection of some deeper non-verbal level and thus can serve as a direct means of communication between myself and the viewer.

All these words, of course, only come after the bowl and necessarily present a more oblique view of the challenge and function of my work than does the bowl itself.

ALAN STIRT
VERMONT, UNITED STATES

Spiral Stairs to Zaccahaeus. The challenge was to make an index spiral carved container with a slight taper upwards. The handle should be set high on the lid and stand alone. Zaccahaeus nut was turned and set on a pedestal to achieve this.

Red Square X Four. The challenge was to make a container which had a top similar to St. Basil's Cathedral in Moscow. The container I wanted needed to have eight spirals in groups of four set in the shape of a pillar.

Captive Pink. The challenge was to make a small size container in a reciprocated pattern. The handle set on the lid I wanted was a piece of pink ivory wood set inside blackwood which resembled sharp teeth.

JON SAUER
CALIFORNIA, UNITED STATES

Spiral Stairs to Zaccahaeus. Ebony, rosewood, Zaccahaeus nut. H. 6" x Diam. 2 1/2"

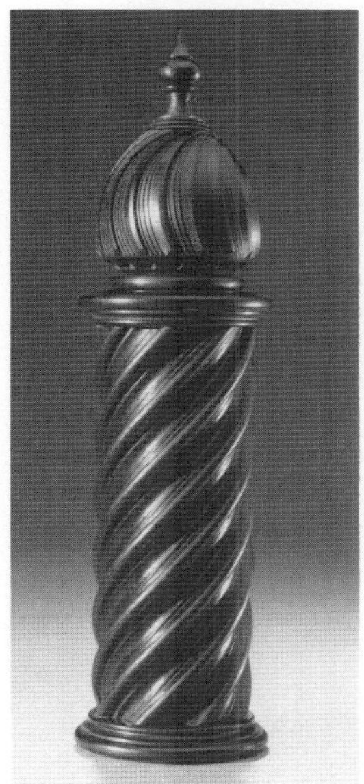

Red Square X Four. Blackwood. H. 6" x Diam. 1 1/2"

Captive Pink. Rosewood, ebony, blackwood, pink ivorywood. H. 5 1/2" x Diam. 2 1/4"

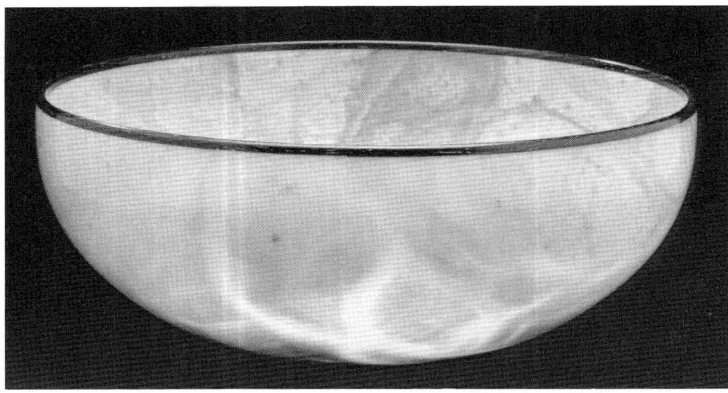

Untitled. Alabaster, cocobolo. H. 3 7/8" x Diam. 9"

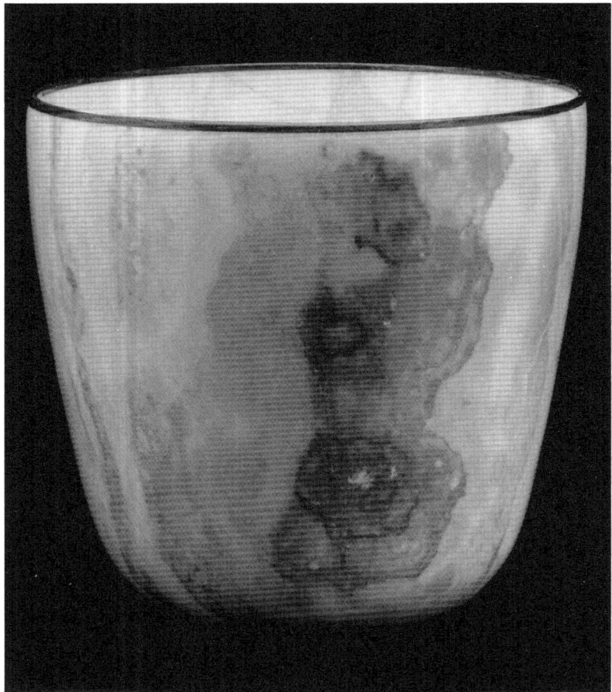

Untitled. Alabaster, cocobolo. H. 10 3/4" x Diam. 10 3/4"

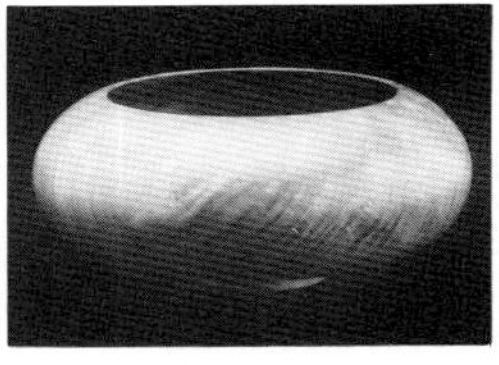

With each of the pieces that I am presenting I have tried to stretch the boundaries of my turning ability and the boundaries of the use of alabaster as a turning medium. The following are statements reflecting some of the challenges that were posed by the specific works.

Untitled . Alabaster bowl. When I turned this piece it was the largest object, in wood or stone, that I had attempted. Vibration at the lip increased as the walls grew thinner, so the challenge came to be achieving the desired consistent wall thickness without shattering the rock. I never actually measured the walls, as I prefer instead to take them down to where I am pleased with the amount of light that passes through.

Untitled. Alabaster vessel. This piece presented as much a mental as a physical challenge. Physically, the weight of the rock when I mounted it on the lathe, in the neighborhood of 125 pounds, was daunting enough. The effort then became more mental since standing in front of an object that size, spinning and unbalanced, held in place basically by a glue joint, is harrowing. Shaping and hollowing were difficult due to the many quartz crystals within the stone, several of which are still visible. These crystals immediately take the edge off a tool, but digging them out with the lathe stopped incurs the risk of cracking or punching a hole in the vessel. On the mental side, taking the walls down to final thickness was a battle between good sense saying "stop before the whole thing blows up" and determination to complete a piece of which I could be proud. I'd like to say that the piece is paper-thin and light as a feather. It isn't. But I enjoy the glow and the colors of the vessel.

ANDREW MACDONALD
COLORADO, UNITED STATES

Wood is the most exquisite of all materials. One can sense that nature herself has created fantastic visual and sensual beauty in wood.

The exciting quest is to reveal this beauty hidden in the wood, and to attempt to discover those utterly simple shapes or forms which will display this beauty without distracting from it and without imposing conflicting shapes or designs upon the beauty which is already there.

It can be said that each bowl already exists in the trunk of the tree, and one's job is simply to uncover it and somehow chip away the excess wood, much as you would chip away the surrounding stone to uncover a perfect fossil entombed in the stone. Thus not only simple shapes, but a search for a crystal clear finish, or special polishings, can be aimed at best revealing the myriad complexities, the subtle or exotic range of colors, and the etching-like patterns of growth rings which nature has placed there in this amazing block of almost homogeneous material which has grown miraculously as a living material.

These feelings about wood, guide me as I work with wood. The lathe and tools, important but not an end in themselves, become a means of expressing the special quality that is "wood."

Ed Moulthrop
Georgia, United States

Forty Inch Banded Bowl. Tulipwood. H. 36" x Diam. 40"

Blackwood Box with Sapwood and Gold. Trying to obtain African blackwood with at least some sapwood in the surface from overseas mills has been a frustrating and unrewarding effort. I finally had to cut up a 900-pound log, obtaining less than a dozen pieces with interesting sapwood presentation. This was the only piece in which two separate parts of the surface were mixed with sapwood. The ornament is a phase-inverted variation of my favorite rose engine rosette around a gold inlay.

Merry Christmas 1990: Charlotte Box. This box was conceived as a Christmas present for my wife and became, I feel, the best piece of my career. It was the most amazing piece of parakingwood, severely cracked and littered with defects. Over twenty hours were necessary to deal with the defects, and yet some remain. It was worth it as this is a truly unique piece of parakingwood.

The spiderweb pattern of the ornament has become known as a *Charlotte Box.* The scale of the ornament seems to mate well with the size of the piece and the grain of this most unusual wood, yielding my most rewarding piece to date.

It was presented to my wife during the 19th year of our marriage. I hope to grow in this effort each year.

M. Dale Chase
California, United States

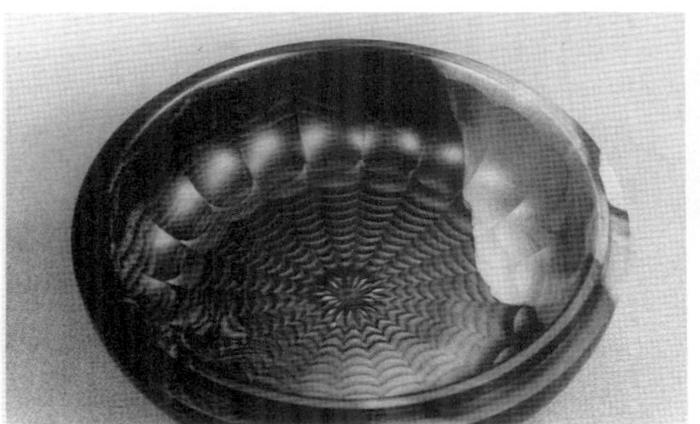

Merry Christmas 1990: Charlotte Box. Parakingwood. H. 2 3/4" x Diam. 4 1/4"

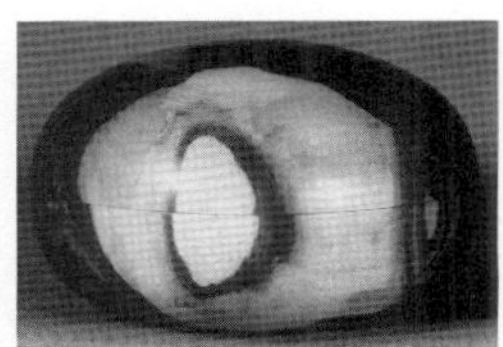

Second view: closed box.

Blackwood Box with Sapwood and Gold. African blackwood, gold. H. 1 1/2" x Diam. 3"

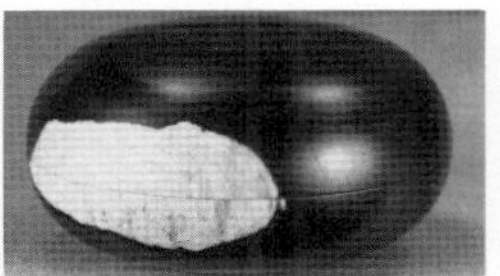

Second view: closed box.

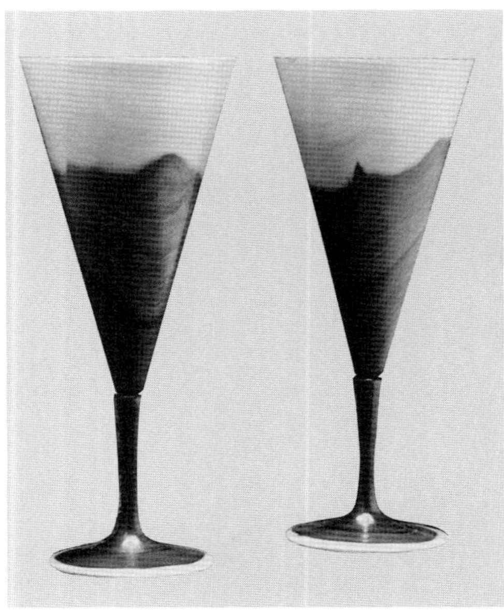

Translucent Goblets. Cereipo (Venezuela).
H. 7" x Diam. 3"

For me, basic art should be life style. From that point, functional items should be artistic in the way of exciting your senses.

As wine qualities work on subtle level of senses, the good wine goblet interferes as little as possible between you and your wine.

Wood is warm and sensual to your eyes and skin (hand and lips).

The very fine wood goblets are weightless and by flexibility, almost unbreakable.

For these characteristics, they very little interfere in the appreciation your wine; no coldness or hardness, no extra weight and none stress usable.

But trying is the only way to really understand what it means.

ANDRE MARTEL
QUEBEC, CANADA

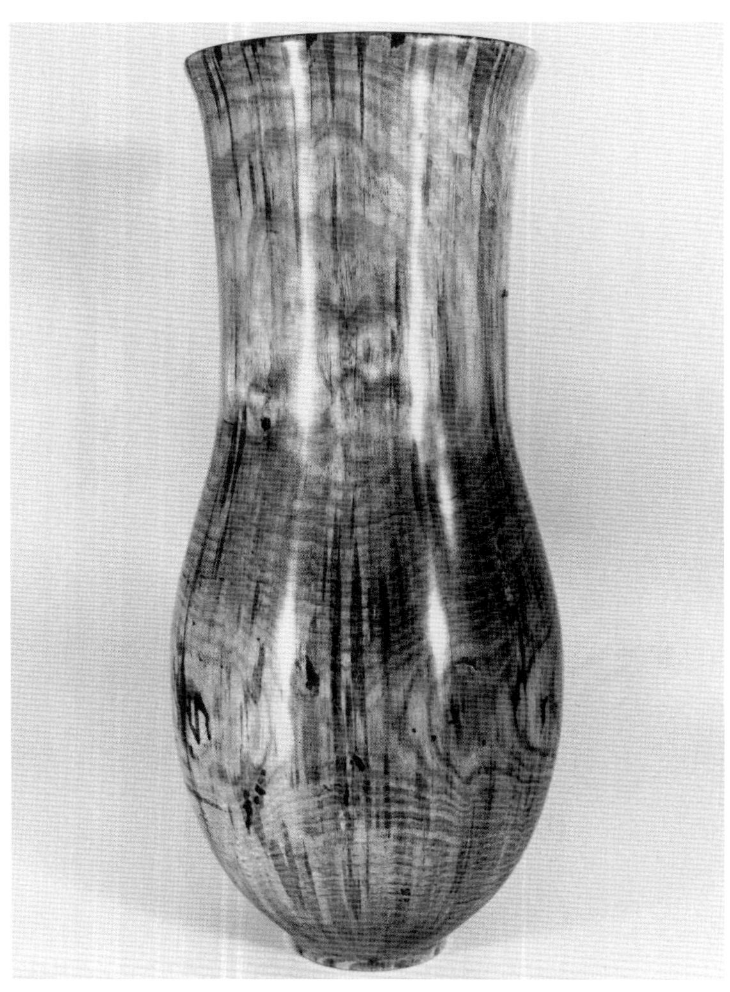

Streaked Pine Vase. Yellow pine. H. 37 1/2" x Diam. 16"

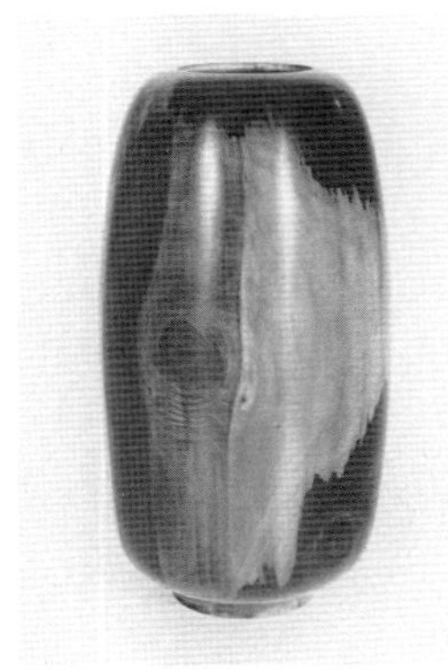

This piece was a challenge in its size alone. The mass of the wood along with the fact that it was turned while suspended from one end made for difficult turning.

PHILIP MOULTHROP
GEORGIA, UNITED STATES

CHAPTER TWO:

BEFORE AND AFTER LATHE WORK

I began working on a turned design box with hinged doors in 1988. "Hidden Treasure" is the seventh such box. It was a challenge to carry a successful concept even further. Previous boxes had two doors with three or four trays. This box is larger, with four doors instead of two, with five trays instead of three or four and has a fourth "dummy" hinge/latch for symmetry.

"Hidden Treasure" consists of 23 individual turnings. I like the way the simple shape and black and white appearance of the closed box contrasts with the bright color and surprising effect of the opened box. The mechanics of the design are very satisfying to my personal fascination with wooden mechanisms.

RAY JONES
NORTH CAROLINA, UNITED STATES

Hidden Treasure. Finland birch plywood, ebony, padauk. H. 7 1/4" x Diam. 10"

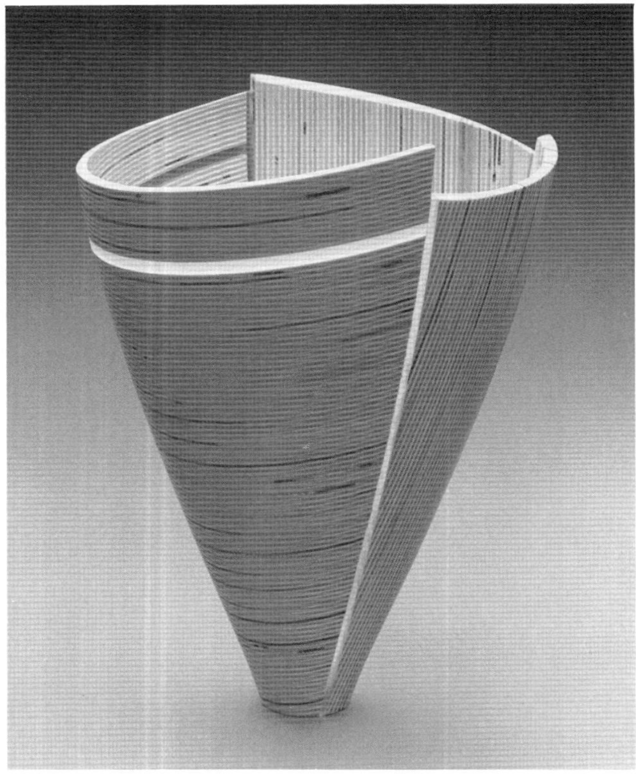

Memory Of The Sea. Baltic birch, acrylic. H. 12" x Diam. 9"

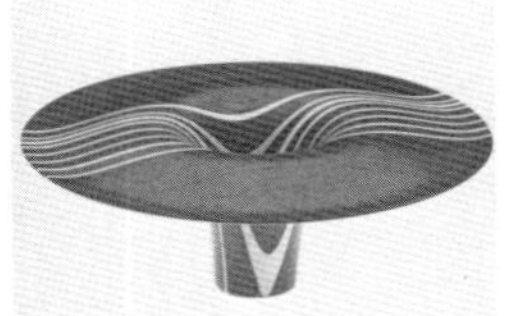

Memory of the Sea. To create this piece, I had to use what I know in other fields and integrate it with turning. The theme of this vessel evolved from an earlier sculpture, and the awareness of light comes from my work in photography.

Dunes Series, #5. This piece represents another departure from the one-way linear patterns of my earlier work.

Calligraphy. In laminated work, each new design requires its own structure. The structure must be appropriate for the material of which it is made. The properties of Baltic Birch are not the same as natural wood, and the greater freedom of the material made possible this structure which interacts freely with the turned form.

VIRGINIA DOTSON
ARIZONA, UNITED STATES

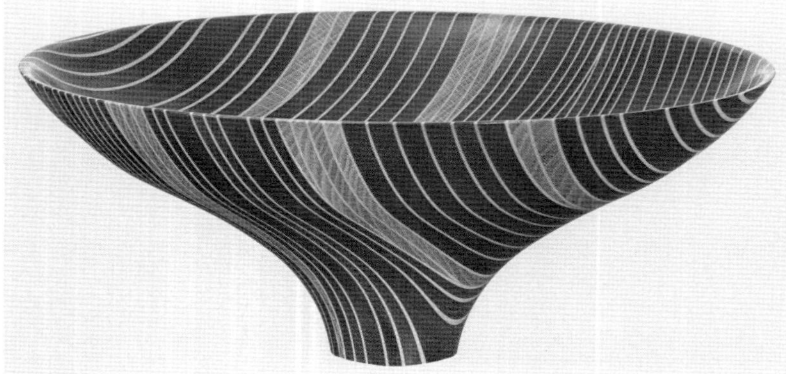

Dunes Series,#5. Purpleheart, white oak, maple. H. 5 3/4" x Diam. 13 1/4"

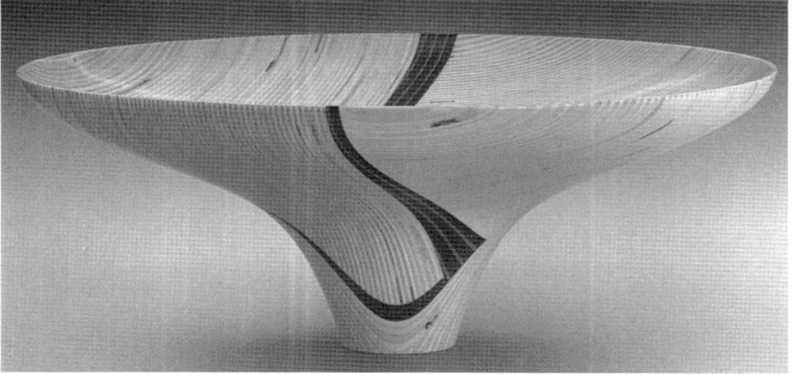

Calligraphy. Baltic birch, wenge, walnut. H. 5 3/4" x Diam. 14 3/4"

PAUL CLARE
DYFED, WALES

Thistle Head Pot. Xanthorea. H. 8 1/2" x Diam. 8 1/2"

[See photo of earlier work on page 35.]

After etching many turned bowls with a sandblasting technique, the thought occurred to me that it would be interesting to pierce through by etching out the soft grain totally and leave the hard grain.

Douglas fir was used in this case because it has alternating very hard and very soft grain structure. (Commonly known as annual growth rings.)

Other woods besides fir have been used with this piercing technique such as redwood and Sitka spruce.

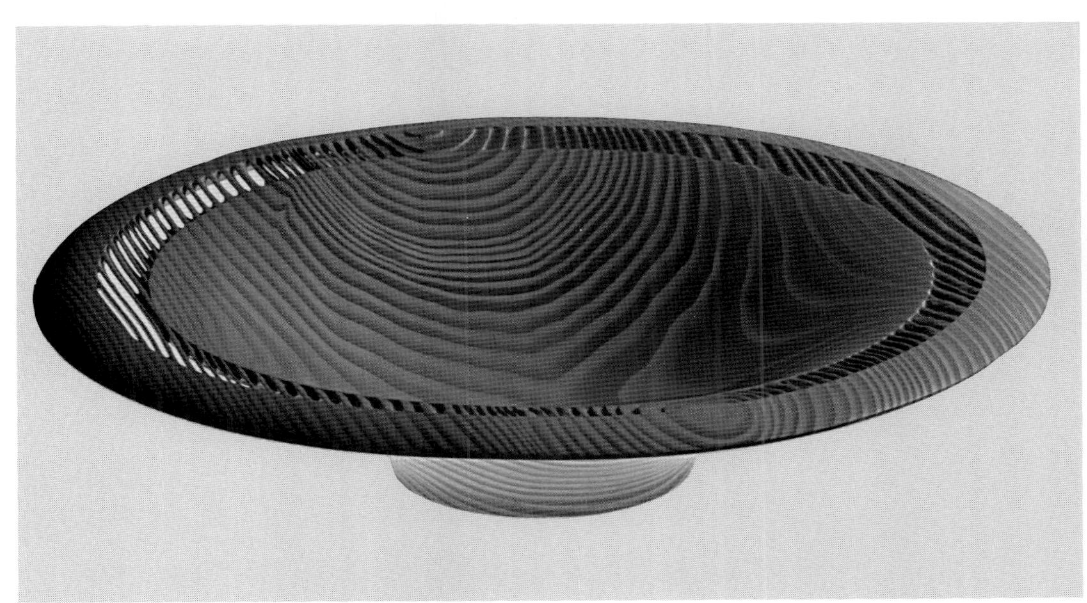

Out Of Africa. Douglas fir. H. 3 1/2" x Diam. 16 1/2"

ALBERT CLARKE
CALIFORNIA, UNITED STATES

Untitled. Figured ash. H. 3 3/4" x W. 9 1/2" x D. 8"

Sometimes looking for the right words is like searching for just that certain curve a bowl should take. There are thousands of possibilities –most of them wrong. I want a piece to reveal something–about the tree it was, about the wood itself, about the turning process. If I am successful, it will reveal something of myself as well. These elements are of equal importance to me–if any one becomes primary, the piece seems unbalanced, not in harmony. Sometimes this harmony is difficult to find. Each block of wood comes to me with a particular history. The piece which comes from it should express many elements of that history. This may mean that I must depart sometimes dramatically from my original idea. I must listen as well as speak. What is this piece trying to say? In this sense, each piece is a new puzzle which must be worked out bit by bit. It is always a struggle, often frustrating or even painful; occasionally exhilarating. It is delightful when a piece gives voice to a grace and equilibrium which seem so impossible to attain elsewhere in life.

JUDY DITMER
OHIO, UNITED STATES

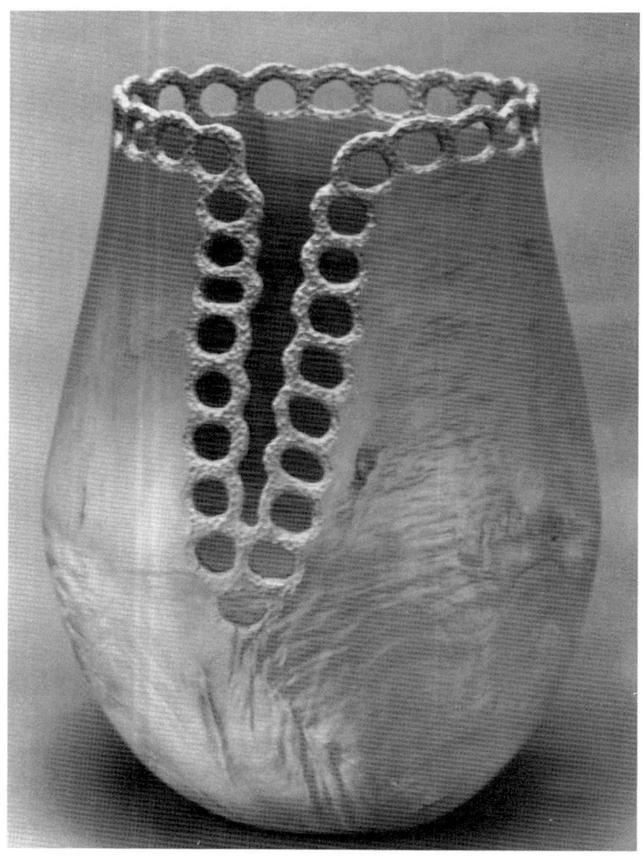

Untitled. Red maple stump. H. 18" x Diam. 12"

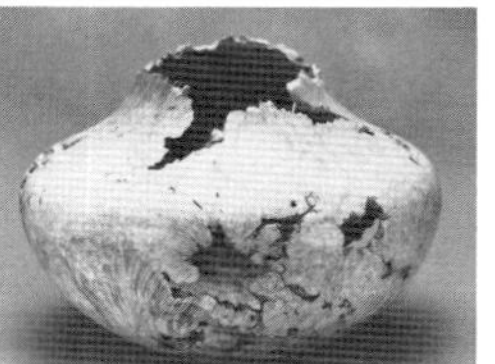

CLEAD CHRISTIANSEN
UTAH, UNITED STATES

The challenges associated with this vessel occur in both the design and execution of the work. The preliminary construction — cutting, fitting, and gluing of plugs to make a blank — must be done with great accuracy and precision. The turning and finishing require extreme care and delicacy. The design challenge is to achieve a pleasing shape with graceful curves that complement the patterns formed by the concentric circular forms. With these vessels, sketches and preliminary ideas can help, but I find that the best shapes are arrived at by trial and error and frequent examination of the work in progress.

Vessels of the *Flower* series impose a number of challenges which must be met to make each form unique. Design choices for the number of petal rings, the number of petals within each ring, the vertical spacing of the rings, and the alignment of the rings must combine to make a pleasing and regular pattern. Similarly, the shape of the bowl and its coloring must add to the effect of the patterns of petals. In this work, I bleached the finished parts to obtain a lighter white color and incorporated a bright contrasting ring of padauk to accent the rim. These vessels are challenging in the precision sizing required and in the careful work needed to turn the delicate rings of petals.

The vessels of the *Lattice* series are difficult and challenging, but for me, the results are usually worth the risks entailed. The preparatory stages involving the glue-up of slats, spacers, and fillers is tedious but critical in that a single poor glue joint will allow the bowl to come apart while turning due to centrifugal force and the forces of cutting. The turning of the prepared blank is very demanding and risky. Very light cuts must be taken with very sharp tools to avoid a catch and the resulting instantaneous disassembly. The lathe must be very solid and steady and my concentration must be tightly focused on the work at hand. The artistic challenge for this bowl is the need to visualize the finished work for the interaction of the slats and spaces and the moire' patterns that will be revealed. This visualization comes only with the experience of making many vessels and experimenting with shapes and designs.

Dewey N. Garrett
California, United States

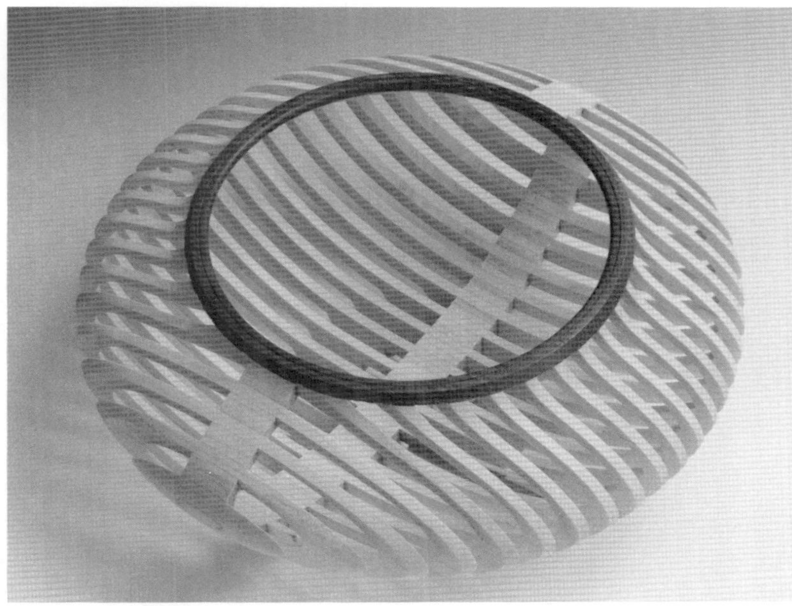

Serene Moiré. Maple, padauk. H. 4" x Diam. 9"

Walnut Petal Vessel. Walnut. H. 3" x Diam. 9"

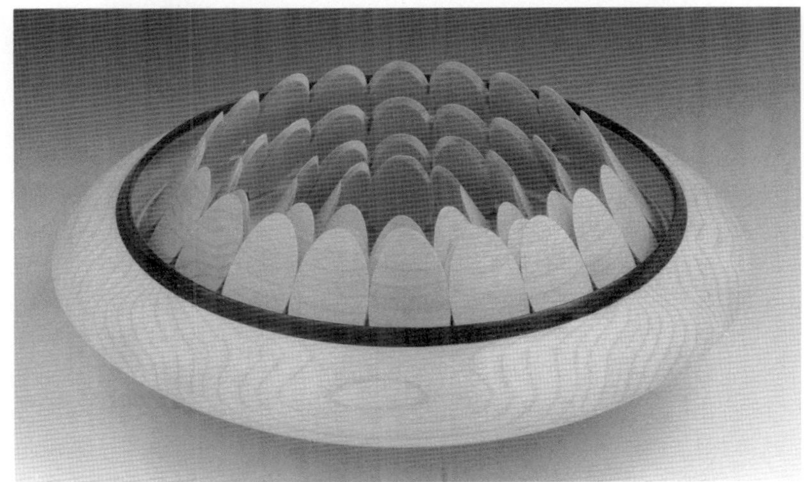

Opening #3. Maple, padauk. H. 3" x Diam. 10"

Petals. Spalted maple. H. 3 1/2" x Diam. 11"

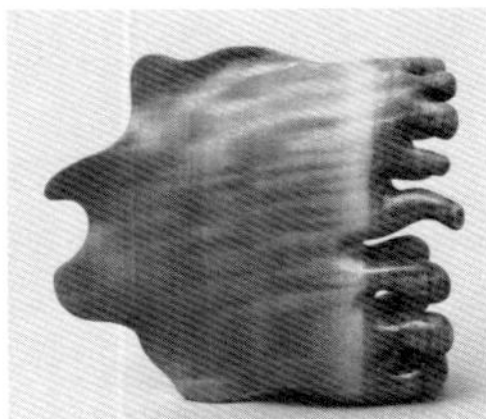

The personal challenge for me in this piece was to create an organic line from a symmetrical edge and delineate the figure in the wood grain. The mental picture before turning was of a flower. It was also my intention to connect the wood to its organic roots by allowing a rigid material to become flowing.

MELINDA FAWVER
CALIFORNIA, UNITED STATES

Lacewood Vessel. Lacewood, bog oak. H. 17" x Diam. 10"

This vessel in lacewood represents my latest designs with large double rims. More important for me than a contrived design, the form just seemed to flow from the unconscious. One day I was turning classical shaped vases, the next... The challenge [continues to be] refining the form and technique.

MELVYN FIRMAGER
SOMERSET, ENGLAND

In addition to texture, color–the use of finely detailed lid to enclose space inside.

"Let the work speak for itself, or sing if it can."
— David Pye

JOHN JORDAN
TENNESSEE, UNITED STATES

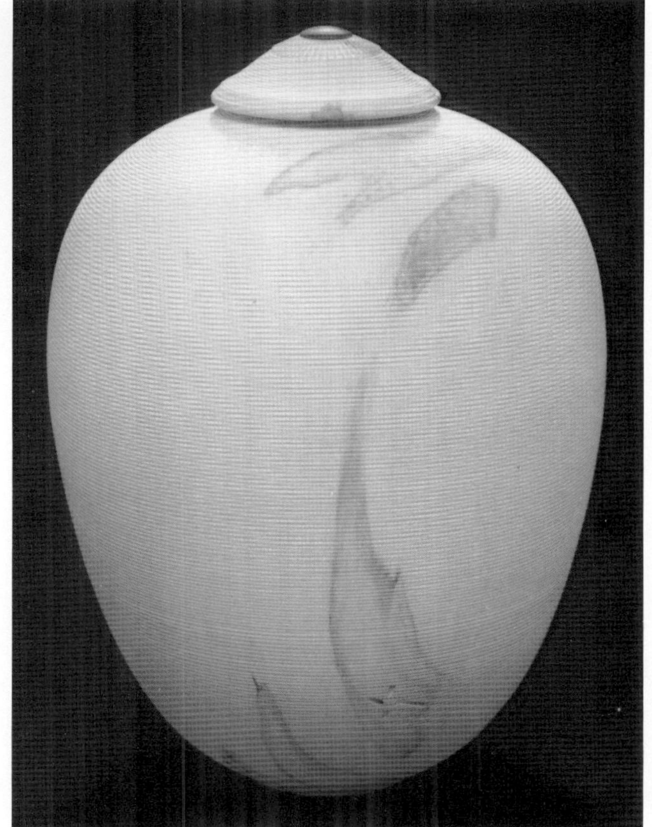

Textured Jar. Bleached box elder, pink ivorywood. H. 11" x Diam. 9"

Basket IX is the first in the basket series to incorporate patinaed copper in the design. We have tried to progress with each piece in this series . . . *Basket IX* represents a more widespread use of metal in all of our work.

CHARLES AND TAMI KEGLEY
TEXAS, UNITED STATES

Basket IX. Basswood, copper. H. 9" x Diam. 12"

19

Recycled Metal Series. Black walnut, brass, colored epoxy resin.
H. 3 1/2" x Diam. 14 1/2"

Current work is still part of an on-going material investigation which began in 1985. My concept has been to utilize the embedding of natural or dyed linear elements and metals, in concert with a variety of colored epoxy resins, to produce an additional element of surface energy onto turned wooden vessels.

The series that I am working on now is attempting to recycle metals that I have picked up in local scrap yards. The challenge here has not only been how to turn these materials on a wood lathe but how to achieve impregnation of the metals with resin. It has been a technical labyrinth which has slowly been overcome. My pile of rejects though has been growing and growing.

DAVID LOEWY
ONTARIO, CANADA

Large Bowl. Mahogany, tulipwood, dyed veneers. H. 7" x Diam. 22"

Large Bowl. is one of the latest in a continuing series of very large bowl forms emphasizing the two natural foci of the form, i.e. the rim and foot. In this piece the negative curve of the sculpted foot flexes against the sweeping curve of the bowl. The segmented rim reveals the end grain of a single plank of tulipwood framed in the contrasting primary colors of dyed veneers. Turned down to average thickness of 0.150", the bowl weighs in at just over 950 grams.

BARRY T. MACDONALD
MICHIGAN, UNITED STATES

I have never used any other media in combination with my wood vessels. My personal challenge was to incorporate other media to create a new look.

Indian Food Jar was a Southwest Indian handmade look.

LANE PHILLIPS
UTAH, UNITED STATES

Indian Food Jar. Boxelder burl, muledeer antler.
H. 4 1/4" x Diam. 7 1/2"

After Monet. The interior of this piece is a pool. A clear pool with shafts of light piercing it and the challenge was to control the surrounding coloring to enhance this watery quality. The final effect was so impressionist that the title was inevitable.

Rim Series. Before this piece I had only "coloured" wood using an oxyacetylene torch to scorch the wide rim in contrast to the pale vessel. It was a considerable challenge to apply colour and movement in a way that blended with, and enhanced, the subtle beauty of this wood.

GAEL MONTGOMERIE
DUNEDIN, NEW ZEALAND

After Monet. Sycamore, acrylic paint, willow twigs. H. 3 1/2" x Diam. 15"

Rim Series. Sycamore, acrylic paint. H. 4 3/4" x Diam. 13 1/2"

The ball-box is my special thing. Normally I turn it from one piece of wood. But it looks better when I take two kinds of wood.

Second view: closed.

HANS J. WEISSFLOG
HILDESHEIM, WEST GERMANY

Ball-Box, Turned Broken Through. Grenadill, boxwood. Diam. 2"

Pomegranate Time. Maple, walnut, sterling silver.
H. 3 1/4" x W. 3" x D. 2 3/4"

Pomegranates (*Punica granatum*) are famous for one thing: their seeds. They have loaned their name to the explosive grenade (from the Old French grenade, a pomegranate), possibly because of their reputation for literally bursting with seeds. My challenge in exploring this form was to produce recognizable (though not literal) examples of the species without actually having to make all those little seeds. I have tried to hint at their multitudinous presence through the pattern on the silver doors, and through the interior carving. Other aspects of the form - its more or less hexagonal cross-section, variations in the appearance of the blossom and stem ends, the way the seeds push against the thin skin from beneath it to give the fruit its exterior shape - are treated in a more straightforward manner.

The work was a technical challenge, not only because of the accuracy with which both wood and metal pieces had to fit in order for the pomegranates to function as intended, but also because I had little knowledge of hinges and catches when I began to design the hardware. An antique pocket watch inherited from my grandfather-in-law gave me some ideas for coping with these elements, and this relationship of watch to fruit is reflected in the work's title.

LOTTIE KWAI LIN WOLFF
CONNECTICUT, UNITED STATES

Pomegranate Time. Maple, cherry, sterling silver.
H. 3 1/8" x W. 3" x D. 2 3/4"

Weed Pot evolved from a continuous fascination with the elements of nature. The bowl, with it's roots, became the substance of the tree growing above the ring of ground level. Wild cherry accepted the carving necessary to make the tree and it's below ground roots realistic.

Weed Pot #1. Wild cherry. H. 4 1/2" x Diam. 3 1/2"

ROBERT F. SALMONSEN
PENNSYLVANIA, UNITED STATES

Although I turn a variety of objects, I invariably return to laminated work because I find this form of turning particularly rewarding.

Unlike turning a solid piece of wood, where one must work within the physical constraints of a particular piece, laminated turnings allow greater freedom to explore the many facets of plastic elements in design. By cutting wood and reassembling them, one can work not only with defining line and form, but also decorative elements by combining different kinds and shapes of wood.

Ideas for design can often come from unlikely places. I saw a decorative brick fence not long ago where the bricks were spaced apart to give a pierced look. I worked this effect into a turning and it is the basis for my latest series of vessels.

Harlequin I. Padauk, Brazilian satinwood. H. 5 1/2" x Diam. 5 1/4"

YOSH SUGIYAMA
CALIFORNIA, UNITED STATES

Petrified Market Basket. Ipê, zebrawood, amapa, black dyed birch. H. 17" x W. 15" x D. 9"

Petrified Banquet Basket. Various hardwoods. H. 3" x Diam. 25"

Petrified Shopping Basket. Ipê, cherry.
H. 18" x W. 15" x D. 9"

Petrified Market Basket. The primary challenge here was to extend the basket illusion concept from just a turned segmented assembly to a segmented form, in which turned and otherwise-fashioned parts, both real and illusory, are merged in an aesthetically compatible context.

The secondary challenge was to create the shadows necessary to blend the real and illusory portions.

Petrified Banquet Basket. The main challenge here was to extend the basket illusion concept to include a wall hanging form, in which the aesthetic interest dominates both the form and the illusion.

Secondary challenges were technical; namely, to overcome turning vibration due to asymmetrical distribution of woods of differing weight-densities, and to rebuild my lathe to avoid its innate size and speed control limitations.

Petrified Shopping Basket. The secondary challenge was methodological, namely to find a practical way to accurately assemble over 5,000 pieces. The problem was solved with the use of the heretofore untried polychromatically-assembled-stave construction.

LINCOLN SEITZMAN
NEW JERSEY, UNITED STATES

Chapter Three:
The Manipulated Image

The initial idea: a form folded/molded from a flat piece of material. The turned form consists of a bowl within an outer ring of solid wood, triangular in cross-section. First sketches, done directly on the turned form, were of evenly-spaced pleat-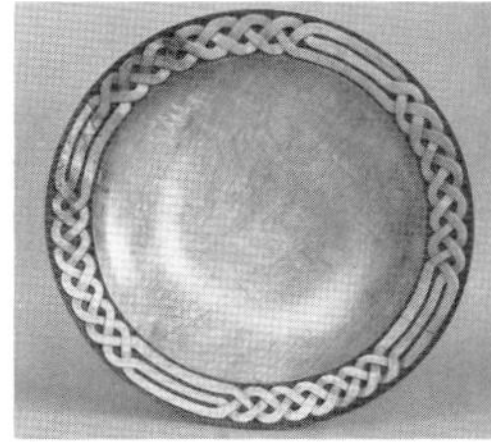ing. The interruption of natural flaws in the wood, however, gave impetus to further consideration before carving. I played with stretching and/or compressing the pleats to generate a rhythm, and settled on beginning the form at the natural cleft with pleating gradually stretching to a curve. It has the rhythm of a clock winding down.

The stippled/burnt corduroy texture on the reverse enhances the textile feeling, and the highly-polished center contrasts. It's pleasing to discover that this piece stands on edge, which emphasizes the clock reference.

Opportunities to envision, to trust my instincts, to develop and realize my intent spring from the combination of planning and improvisation that is the pleasure of making.

Michelle Holzapfel
Vermont, United States

Time Piece. Beech burl. H. 15" x W. 15" x D. 3 1/2"

Mana, as the title suggests is based on the flowing skirt/wings of the Mana Ray. The flowing lines and the sense of movement is what I am trying to achieve in this work.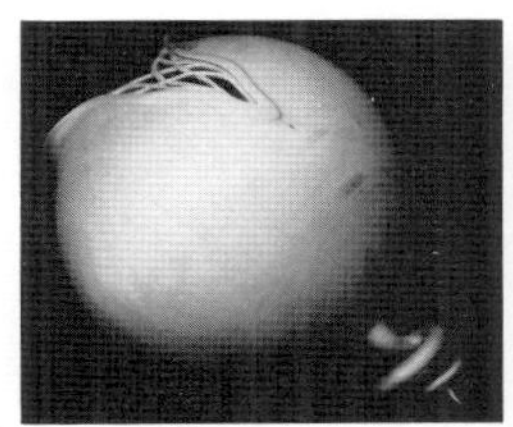

The epoxy legs are brass pinned into the huon pine bowl form and they have been added to lift the bowl and hold it in suspension—the illusion of the floating form being free of gravity and drifting in space has become one of my goals in this work. Turned and carved, the work is a culmination of my 12 years experience as a wood artist.

Stephen Hughes
Mordialloc, Australia

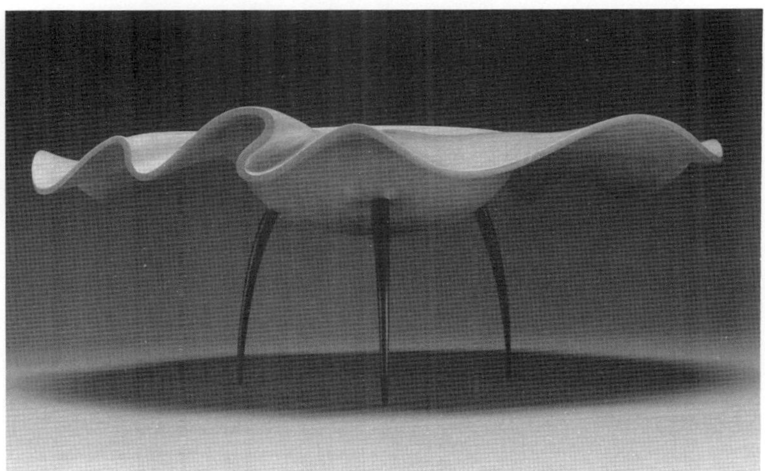

Mana. Huon pine, brass, Indian ebony. H. 6 3/4" x Diam. 18 1/2"

OME. White ash. H. 16" x W. 16" x D. 16"

The *Solstice Series* represents an effort to expand beyond the vessel forms of my previous work, to re-connect with the universal motivations for making art and to manifest these concepts into primary forms—in particular, spherical forms. These 'Spheres' symbolize form-in-motion: stationary, but not static, where the surface becomes a canvas for expression through the integration of color, fire and the metamorphosed textures of the material itself. Within these volumes I encounter both spirit and pulse, the origins of force; elements that engender the same qualities of mystery that I find within myself.

DAVID ELLSWORTH
PENNSYLVANIA, UNITED STATES

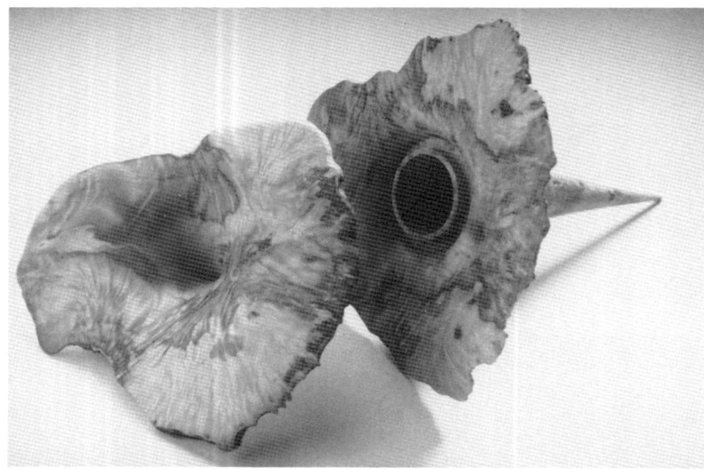

Box, Blossom. Boxwood burl. H. 4" x W. 4 3/8" x D. 5"

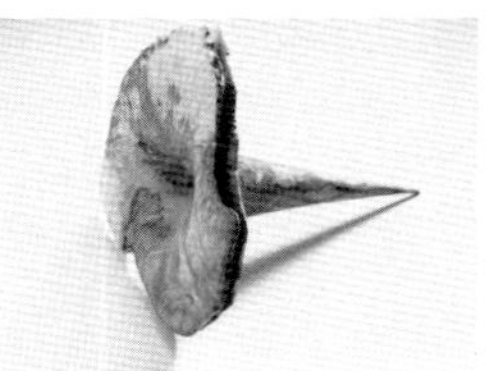

Second view: closed box.

HANS J. WEISSFLOG
HILDESHEIM, WEST GERMANY

CHAPTER FOUR:
THE VESSEL REDEFINED

Up to the present time, the main thrust of my woodturning activity has been interpretations of thin-walled hollow form vessels, mainly in variations of classic forms. Each of these pieces is an end unto itself. For the challenge, I wanted to integrate my woodturning capabilities with another medium and explore their sculptural interrelationship . . . this is an entirely new direction for me.

For the other medium, I am using luminous tubing—typically called "neon"—well-known commercially but relatively new as an art form. Neon by its very nature is a bold visual statement, and these two entries represent my initial attempt of its use with wood. The turnings are simple forms—flower-shaped translucent calyxes, and the neon, a single slightly curved line representing the stamen. The maple wood has been bleached as white as possible so that its translucent characteristics interplay with the neon luminescence.

J. PAUL FENNELL
MASSACHUSETTS, UNITED STATES

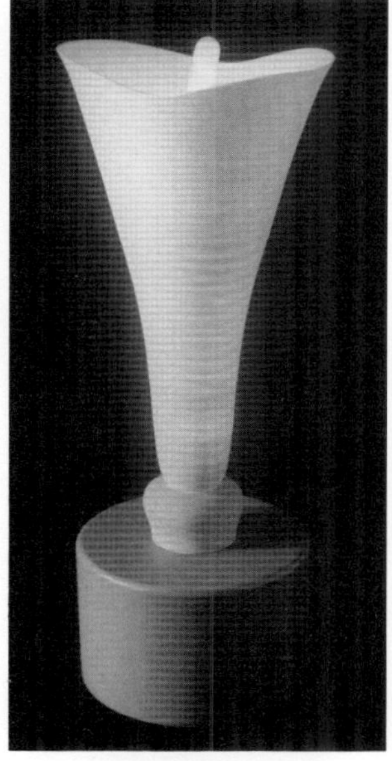

Fleur de Neon I. Bleached curly maple, luminous neon tubing, aluminum base.
H. 11" x Diam. 4"

Fleur de Neon II. Bleached curly maple, luminous neon tubing, aluminum base.
H. 11" x Diam. 4"

Suspended Redwood Flora.
I was trying to achieve a
vessel that is suspended
and balanced with the leaf
forms that I incorporate
into my vessels.

RON FLEMING
OKLAHOMA, UNITED STATES

Suspended Redwood Flora. Redwood burl. H. 6" x W. 10" x L. 21"

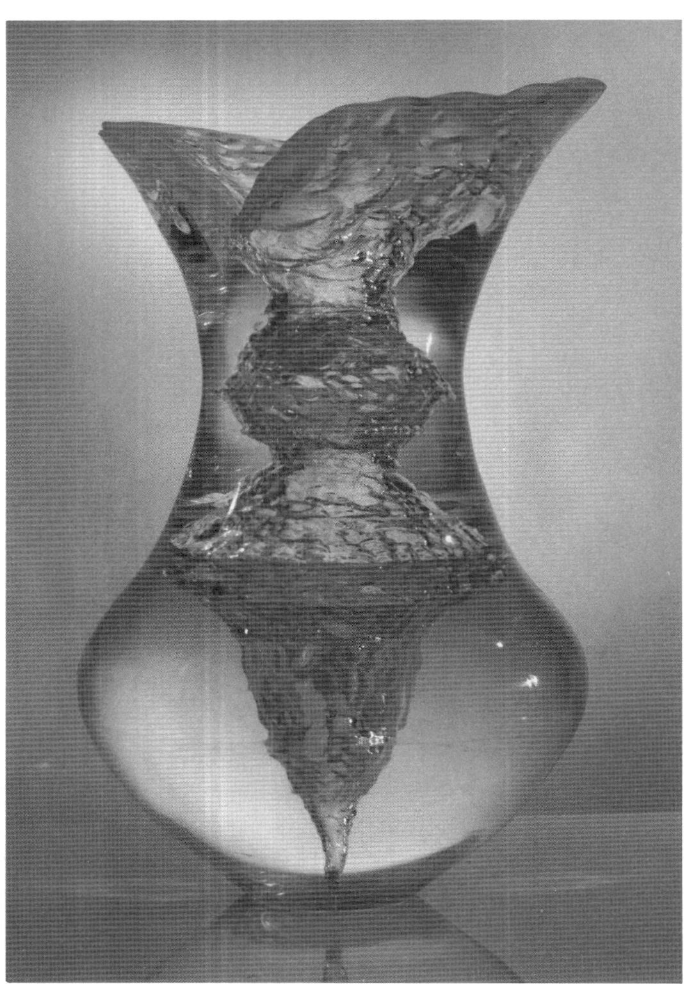

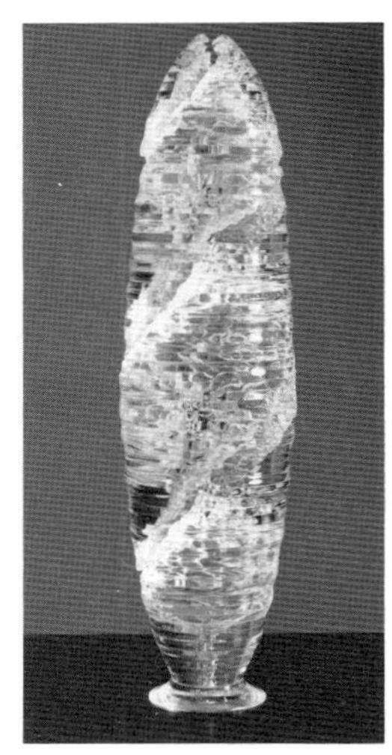

Turning a transparent
medium on the lathe has
posed many exciting
challenges. Plexiglas, to
turn, is heavier than
wood and very brittle.
Optically clear medium
shows no mercy; every
detail is exposed. Uur
design challenge was to
form an inner symbolic
and outer classical form
and to compensate for the
lens action of the outer
shape. Our change in di-
rection with *Lotus Urn*
was to keep the inner
shape continuous, even
though the urn is layered,
and to make the bonding
as seamless as possible.
The object is a sculpture,
a container for flowers, a
collector and transmitter
of light.

MAYA AND TERRY BALLE
MASSACHUSETTS, UNITED STATES

Lotus Urn. Acrylic. H. 18" x Diam. 10"

A Tranquil Moment. This pair of vases is meant to represent a couple having a rare, but desperately needed, quiet moment in a busy life.

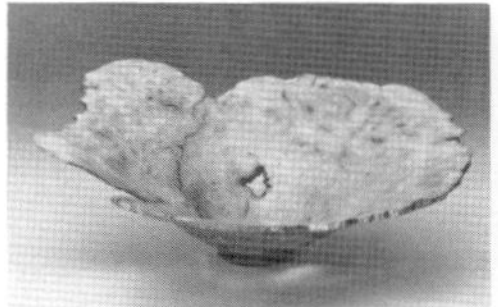

JACK HANSON
PENNSYLVANIA, UNITED STATES

A Tranquill Moment. Maple burl.
H. 14" x W. 16" x D. 8"

Recently I have become interested in metal spinning. This has opened up new possibilities for me. The use of rotational form created in copper, brass or silver combined with turned wood forms has greatly expanded my palette of surface texture and color. In my most recent piece, *Tea Balance*, [see page 60] I have also included turned and carved soap stone. I believe the close proximity of wood, metal and stone increases one's sense of the properties and qualities of each. Using these materials, I am trying to create vessels which go beyond function, that mine the fertile ground of the metaphorical and historical content found in the vessel form.

In viewing the metal artifacts from early civilization, I have been moved by the sense of importance even ordinary objects have. Even a coin or a toga pin shows the caring personalized attention of the maker. It is not the form of these objects, but rather the mood of these objects, a transcendence of function and form, that is the inspiration for this series of vessels.

WILLIAM MOORE
OREGON, UNITED STATES

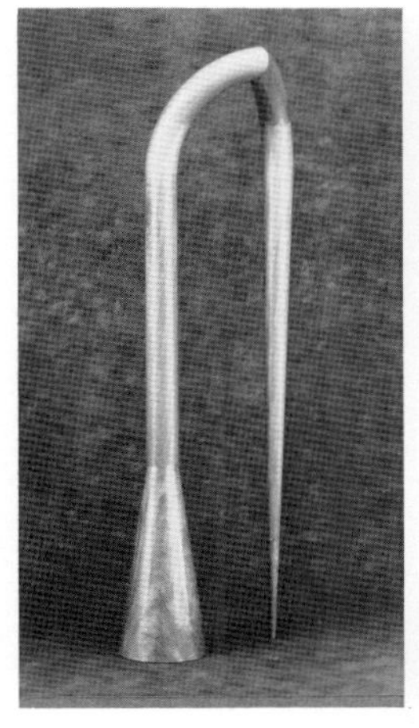

Cumulus. Copper, Western curly maple.
H. 13 1/2" x W. 7" x D. 9"

Timna. Copper, Madrone burl.
H. 10" x Diam. 11 1/2"

CHAPTER FIVE:
BEYOND THE GRAIN

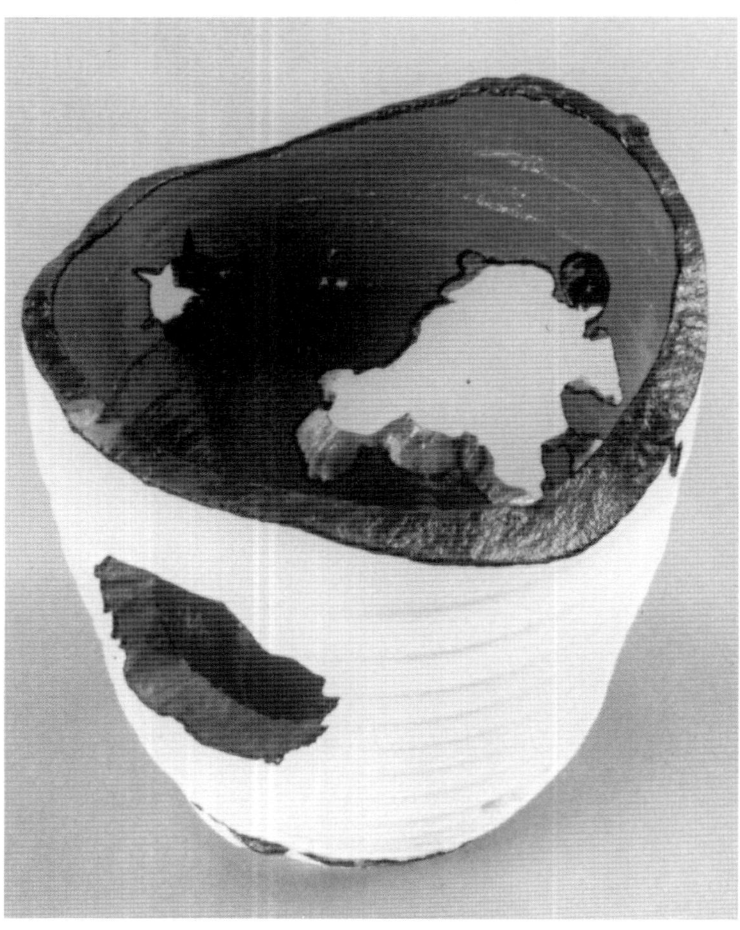

Deep Purple. Cherry, oil based paint, lacquer. H. 9" x Diam. 7"

I had never done a hand painted vessel before. Also the piece had to be sandblasted for texture, which was a new challenge for me.

THOMAS SHERWOOD
PENNSYLVANIA, UNITED STATES

Surfs Up in Pompeii reflects my travels last year. Exposure to new cities, architecture, culture and counterculture.

Surfs Up is from a series called "Unnatural Edge." After turning so many natural edge burl bowls I had to try something different. The outside is painted with casein, the inside dyed.

MICHAEL HOSALUK
SASKATCHEWAN, CANADA

[Photo of earlier work on page 57.]

Surfs Up in Pompeii. Maple burl, casein, dye, copper, horse hair. H. 8 " x Diam. 6"

A new material, a new technique and a new series make *Sea Shell–Fossil Series II* a significant departure from previous work for me.

Continuing to approach the vessel as "object," *Sea Shell*, explores the vessel's rim as an embedded shell-like impression.

MICHAEL PETERSON
WASHINGTON, UNITED STATES

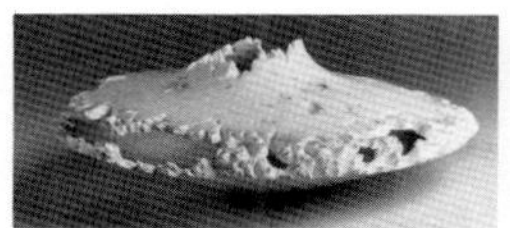

Sea Shell–Fossil Series II. Grass plant. H. 4 1/2" x Diam. 7 1/2"

Top: *Yellow Quilted Maple Bowl.* Quilted maple, transparent yellow lacquer. H. 1 3/4" x Diam. 13 5/8"; Bottom: *Cerise Quilted Maple Bowl.* Quilted maple, transparent cerise lacquer. H. 1 3/4" x Diam. 10 1/2"

Second view: detail of *Cerise Quilted Maple Bowl.*

These two bowls are an attempt to use some of the finishing technology that I have learned through my worked at the Stewart-Macdonald company. I have tried to get the most life out of the quilted maple by using the transparent lacquer to give the figure more depth.

The challenge for me is to turn the wood as thin as I feel comfortable with (usually 1/16" to 1/8") and to apply the lacquer without warping the bowl. At the same time trying to pull the most figure that I can out of the wood while using a simple elegant form.

I used to turn wood to relax but with the new work I have been doing I no longer can. The finishing steps now take longer than the actual turning.

JAY HOSTETLER
OHIO, UNITED STATES

Plate Form #15001. Myrtle, turquoise, brass. H. 1 3/4" x Diam. 11 1/2"

Plate Form #15001. The challenge was to enhance the blemishes in the wood and pull it all together into one composition.

BRENDA BEHRENS
CALIFORNIA, UNITED STATES

[See photo of earlier work on page 28.]

This piece was inspired by the Jipson weed that grows wild in this area.

It is turned from Basswood and primed in gesso.

The object being to combine a full flora painting in airbrush with a form that would support and display such a painting.

The mouth and interior are finished in a high gloss lacquer to contrast the dull exterior.

Datura. Bass wood, acrylic, lacquer. H. 18" x Diam. 21"

RON FLEMING
OKLAHOMA, UNITED STATES

Ceremonial Vessel. Black walnut, maple burl, cobalt pigment.
H. 3" x Diam. 13"

RICHARD SULLIVAN
OREGON, UNITED STATES

Second view: interior.

The Path. Gaboon ebony, abalone, lapiz, malachite, chrolite, rhodochrosite, opal.
H. 2 1/2" x Diam. 8 1/2"

[See photo of earlier work on page 18.]

In this piece, a personal statement is being expressed through inlay. The challenge was to make a decorative pattern also symbolic. The two spirals have a common starting point but extend in opposite directions. This is an analogy, for me, of a person's path in life. One can either lead a closed life (δ) and be restricted and dull, or lead an open life (χ) where there is joy and the possibilities are unlimited.

MELINDA FAWVER
CALIFORNIA, UNITED STATES

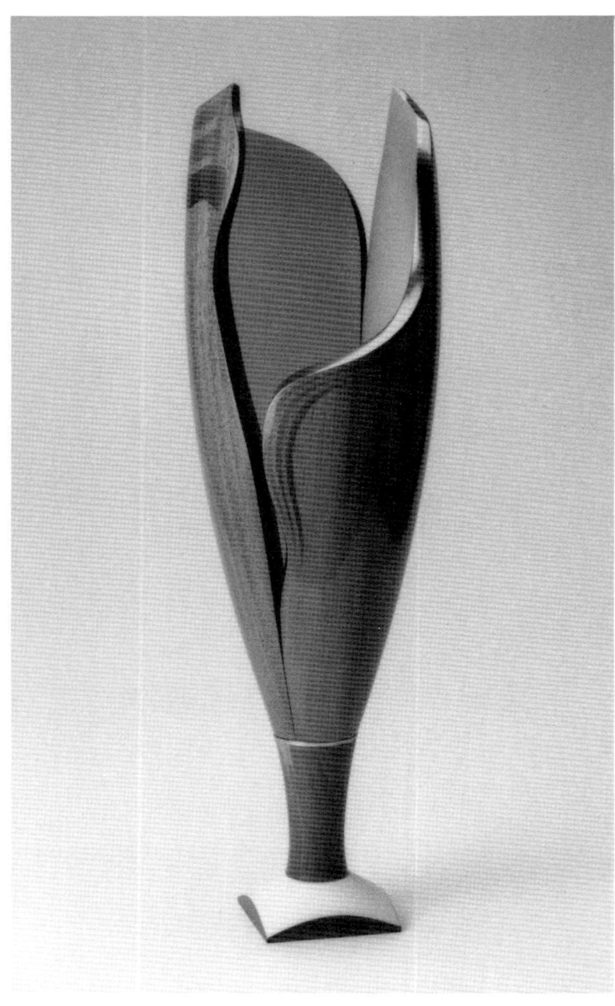

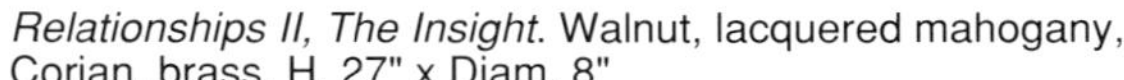

Relationships II, The Insight. Walnut, lacquered mahogany, Corian, brass. H. 27" x Diam. 8"

GILES GILSON
NEW YORK, UNITED STATES

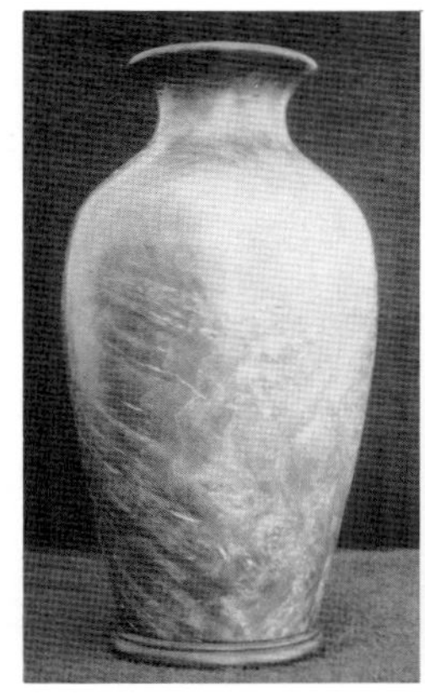

Gift from the Sea is turned from a huge redwood stump that was removed from San Francisco Bay, turned out to be exotic lace burl. . . this accounts for the title. After turning, the bowl was masked with a heavy vinyl tape (resist), and a design was cut forming a stencil.

The bowl was then sand-blasted which tends to etch away the soft grain, leaving the hard grain, emphasizing the exotic lace figuring.

ALBERT CLARKE
MARSHALL, CALIFORNIA

Gift From The Sea. Lace redwood burl. H. 6"x Diam. 15"

After years of using acrylic and nitrocellulose lacquers, I am in search of a way of continuing my use of color with a personally safer and environmentally responsible product. I had been developing my work with suggestions from my wife, Belinda, an accomplished fiber artist. We worked together throughout the development of the form, color and texture of this piece. The result is a true collaboration.

Most of my earlier painted work was a display of graphic images on polished surfaces. This was an exploration of a surface treatment involving both color and texture to enhance the form.

WAYNE AND BELINDA RAAB
NORTH CAROLINA, UNITED STATES

Rice Wispies and Milk II. Maple, waterbase paint, lacquer. H. 10 3/4" x Diam. 8 3/4"

CHAPTER SIX

BEYOND THE BURL

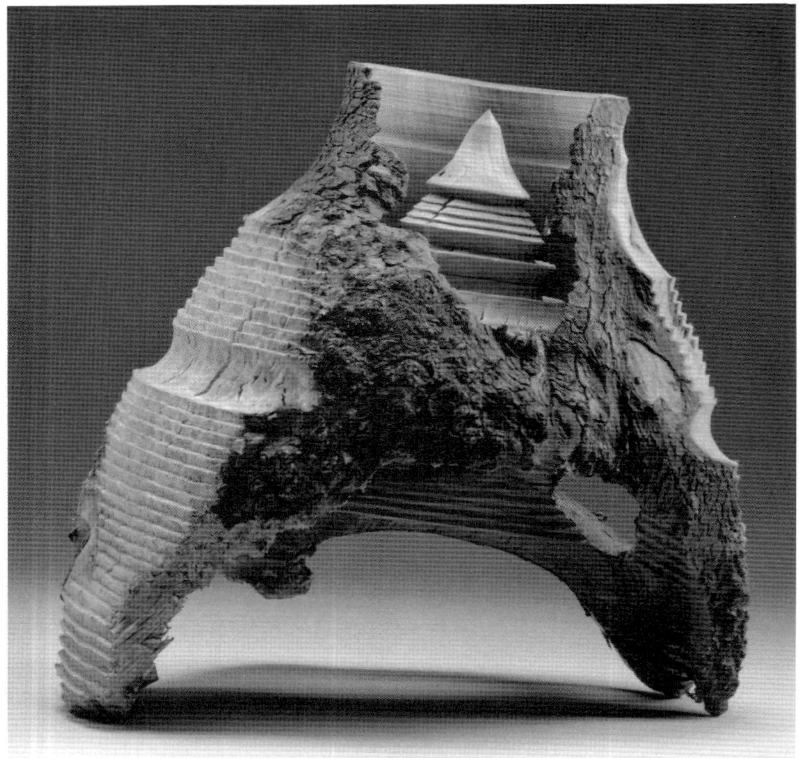

Tomb Of An Unknown King. Madrone stump burl. H. 18" x Diam. 18"

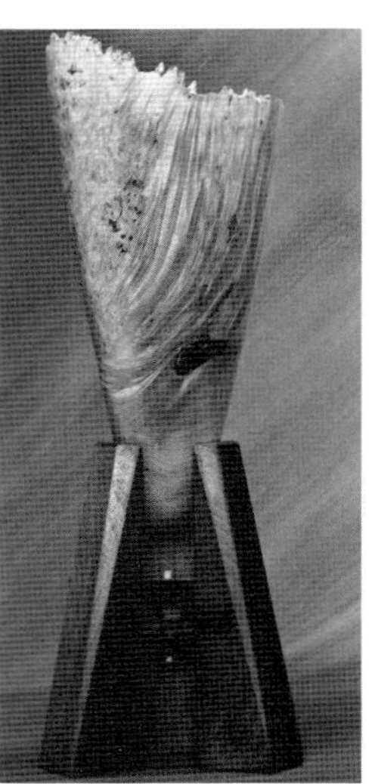

I attempted to explore the surface and the interior of an entire green madrone stump, cut various textures and allowed the wood through loss of its moisture to arrive at its final shape.

CHRISTIAN BURCHARD
OREGON, UNITED STATES

1990 represented a major change in the approach that I took towards my work. Prior to this, the scope of my work was more traditional. Most pieces were variations of bowl or vessel forms. I had not yet begun to experiment with texture and color as design elements and I felt locked into the belief that all surfaces had to be highly finished and polished to prove that I was capable of such "expert finishes." In fact, what I began to prove was that I was boring myself and becoming stagnant.

Therefore, in the past year I have attempted to remove the shackles from my creativity. What followed were objects more sculptural and abstract in form. These forms began to combine contrasting textures, both natural and man-made. I began to experiment with carving, chainsawing, tool marks, scorching and bleaching, and new chucking method, among other techniques.

But most rewarding of all was the growing realization that my avenues of personal expression were nearly limitless!

Viper. My objective with this piece was to turn two pieces and then incorporate them into a single object which, because it was cantilevered, would counter balance itself and stand upright, seeming to defy gravity. I chose to turn a sphere as the bottom section, and use a "crotch" (turned on one side only) as the upper section. This gave the object a combination of natural and machined surfaces. The "snake-like" form was further pursued by carving all machined Surfaces to give the object a "reptilian" feel and appearance.

Human Nature. When I first saw this log lying on a friend's firewood pile, it's "human-like" form struck me almost immediately. My idea was simply to refine this natural form by giving it more uniquely human characteristics, such as a "waist line". In keeping with its theme of "human nature", I finished the turned surface with irregular tool marks by "sliding" the tool across the surfaceat different speeds. The result was a series of irregular and non-aligned grooves which give the piece an imperfect, yet unique unto itself, appearance. The existing "checking" was accelerated by soaking and heating, and these "imperfections" give the piece its most human-like characteristic of all.

DENNIS MUELLER
PENNSYLVANIA, UNITED STATES

Viper. Bleached ash. H. 19" x W. 15" x D. 12"

Human Nature. Bleached maple. H. 32" x W. 18" x D. 8 1/2"

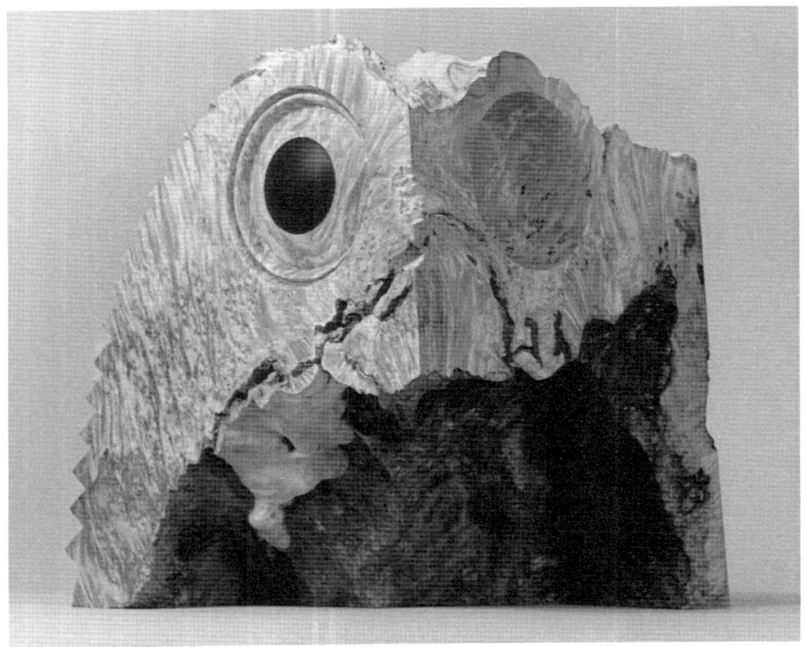

Owl Bowl. Maple, ebony. H. 10 1/2" x W. 9" x D. 8"

The making of the owl challenged me in two ways: As a sculpture of an animate image it marks a definite departure from my past lathe turned pieces, thus challenging my imagination; and on the technical, once seeing the potential in this block of wood the greatest challenge lay in executing it.

I described this piece as a multiple axis turning with a milled surface. Multiple axis because it was turned on three planes necessitating a counter balanced faceplate mounting for each axis.

The curved and faceted milled surface, representational of feathers, was achieved by using a die grinder and end mill bit held in a crossfeed-compound tool rest with the work being rotated past the cutter by hand.

John Macnab
Nova Scotia, Canada

Turned/Free-form Open Bowl. Western maple burl. H. 13 1/2" x Diam. 17 1/4"

My current work has evolved through the exploration of the natural textured surfaces of a variety of burled woods. My attempts to artistically combine the natural textures of the wood with man-made smooth surfaces mirrors the struggle of a peaceful coexistence between nature and humankind. I find challenge in expanding my use of free-from sculpting to highlight attributes of the wood or create visions of nature from the wood.

Turned/Free-form Open Bowl is the result of a personal desire to fuse my distant past of open bowl turning with my more recent work which involves free-form sculpting.

Rod Cronkite
Wisconsin, United States

If it has no possible use ... it must be art.

Sometimes I get a little abstract in my renditions; but I have a reverence for trees, and making a salad bowl from a tree does not say much about the tree, or nature, or anything else . . . So, I don't make salad bowls; I make vessels which say something about hardship, character, and beauty.

JOE DICKEY
MARYLAND, UNITED STATES

Untitled. Weeping willow burl, walnut. H. 9" x W. 25" x D. 16"

Metropolis #3 blends organic and formal, architectural turned elements into an arched form that evokes an image of passage.

STONEY LAMAR
NORTH CAROLINA, UNITED STATES

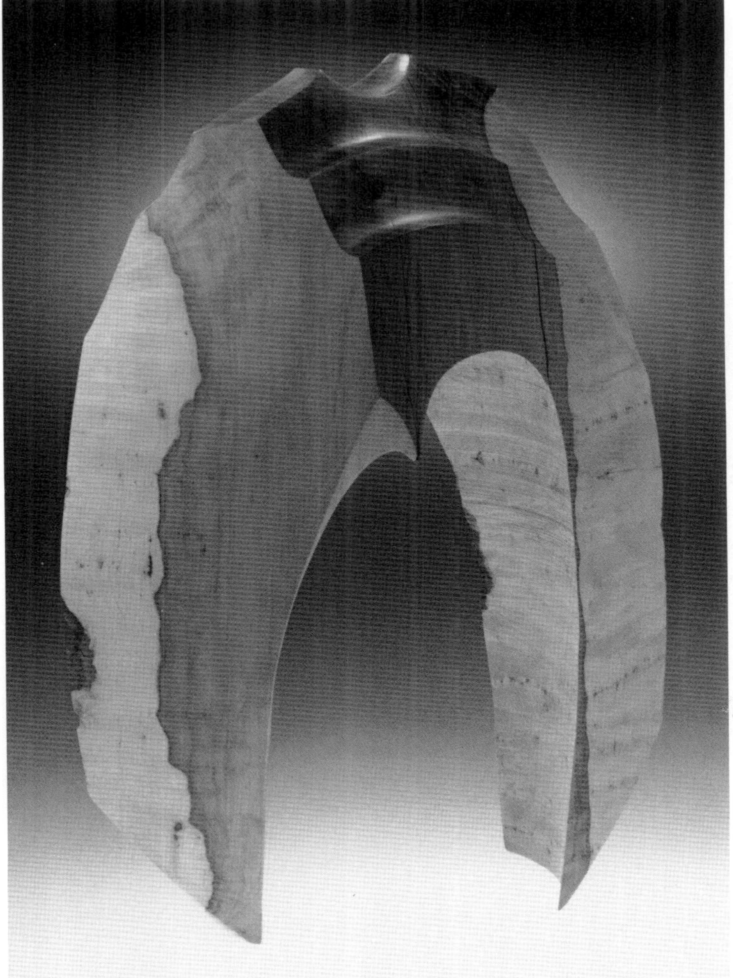

Metropolis #3. Pear. H. 22" x W. 17" x D. 10"

Cherry Burl. Cherry burl. H. 7" x W. 17" x D. 13"

Cherry Burl is based on the *Myrtle Bowl* [shown], working into a larger and more complex scale. I wanted to create an underworld leading into the bowl with remains of the center as its source. This piece challenged me to go slowly and visualize as to where edgers would meet and give way. I wanted this piece to sit with stability, yet with a feeling as if held up by an inner core.

Marcy Dambowic
Florida, United States

Memories of East Texas. Maple, dogwood, oak, birch with paint and dye. H. 9" x W. 17" x D. 8"

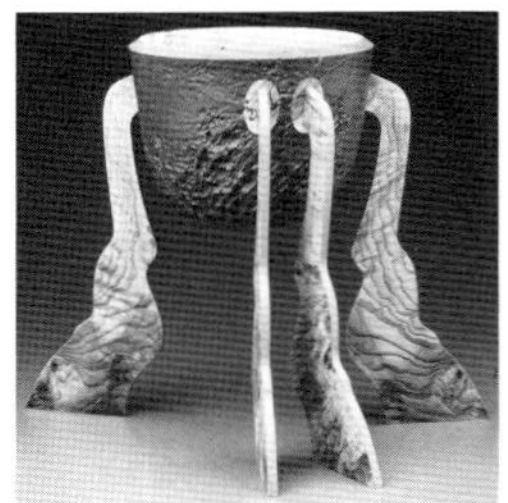

My recent pieces have become sculpture, and were developed by joining cast-off chunks of wood with certain popular songs. A variety of techniques and materials were used in an effort to illicit an intimate emotional response.

Other thoughts are best expressed by other artists:

"My main goal is to make devastatingly beautiful objects."
—Dakota Jackson

"What the audience wants is *not* logic—it is emotion."
—Billy Wilder

"I do all these subtle things, and the world doesn't even notice."
—Alice Neal

Steve Loar
New York, United States

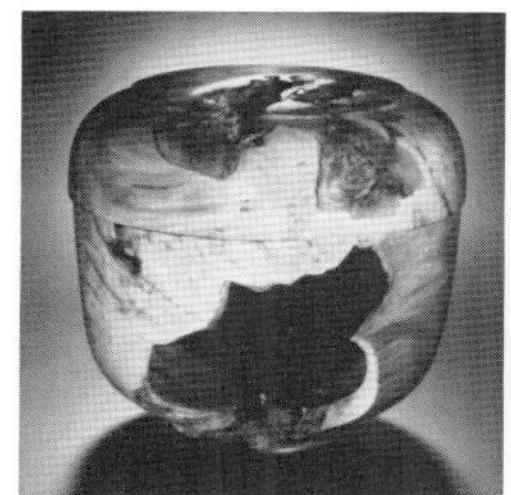

This piece captures the essence of a pigmented epoxy resin inlay technique which I have been working with since 1988. In an attempt to add color to pieces, I originally toyed with painting bowls. However, after using epoxy mixed with sawdust for repair work, it occurred to me that any powdered pigment could be used and that larger areas could be filled. In this piece I paid special attention to the epoxy fill, using metallic powders to create a depth of surface and flow.

ROBERT W. CHATELAIN
VERMONT, UNITED STATES

Untitled. Lilac burl, epoxy resin, powdered pigments, metals. H. 7" x Diam. 8 1/2"

[See photo of earlier work on page 31.]

Fossil I Series. This piece represents my latest approach to the vessel as "object." Employing and exploring surface treatments of bleaching, sandblasting and contouring with lathework, *Fossil I* assumes its final form and definition.

Its suggestive imagery and impressionistic quality are what are important to me and are what I feel make this piece a departure from earlier work.

Fossil I series. Maple burl. H. 5 1/2" x W. 10 1/2" x D. 11 1/2"

MICHAEL PETERSON
WASHINGTON, UNITED STATES

PART TWO

FURNISHINGS

CHAPTER SEVEN

ON THE WALL

The challenge for me remains the same, from day to day, and year to year, from piece to piece; how shall I keep it new? How can I put a new spin on each part of each piece? That's the question that greets me each time I step into the studio. That's the challenge I spend my life rising to meet.

STEPHEN PAULSEN
CALIFORNIA, UNITED STATES

Civilization As They Knew It #5, Catacombs & Fusion Chamber. Various woods, gold leaf and paint. H. 18" x W. 25" x D. 4"

[See photo of earlier work on page 39.]

Resonance has to do with the progression and tone of my work, reflective attitudes that I take about the pieces as a whole, as well as the individual elements in response to each other.

Resonance. Apple. H. 18" x W. 102" x D. 3"

STONEY LAMAR
NORTH CAROLINA, UNITED STATES

This piece was inspired by a trip I took last spring to Italy and Greece. Greece is a land of many layers—the ruins of temples and other buildings everywhere, incorporated and surrounded by the realities of the daily life of the present. The piece is seen from within a room with the vessels, posts and steps in good repair. You look through the doorway to the ruins of a building, just on the other side, not far out of reach.

The vessels are turned wenge, based on the Greek Amphora form. The Amphora was widely used within the ancient Greek culture and represents for me their love of precision and elegance. The form is truly *classical* and has as much strength today as it did then.

ADDIE DRAPER
NEW MEXICO, UNITED STATES

Historical Perspectives. Wenge, ebony, ebonized wood, acrylic, MDF with lacquer finish. H. 28" x W. 30" x D. 3"

Making these *Wall Sculpture* pieces, I feel is a challenge in two respects. First and foremost is the safety factor. I feel that any irregular shape object going round in a lathe is dangerous and the differential in length to width in some of these pieces can be extreme, therefore the first challenge has to be met with a sound technique and a large whiskey!

Second is the challenge of design. Some of the people who encounter these pieces will remark about the shape and I would love to take credit for it but it is purely and simply an act of nature. These slabs come in all shapes and sizes and for me the biggest challenge is in designing within these natural boundaries.

DENNIS ELLIOTT
CONNECTICUT, UNITED STATES

Wall Sculpture. Bigleaf maple burl, pink alabaster, African blackwood, metal. H. 27" x W. 32" x D. 2"

Motor Boat to Mars. Walnut, striped ebony, gold leaf, sterling silver. H. 12 1/2" x W. 16" x D. 3 3/4"

Amid all the controversy of late, that vessels are all too prevalent in the wood turning field, I decided to try a piece of sculpture. Using turning, off-center turning and carving techniques, I arrived at the walnut and striped ebony piece I call *Motor Boat to Mars.* As I sit and ponder the design, material and title of this piece, I realize I have created yet another vessel, but a vessel of another sort, a vessel for flight and fancy.

So I've arrived at the unavoidable conclusion that whether we call sculpture a vessel or a vessel sculpture they are all in fact, both.

JOHANNES MICHELSEN
VERMONT, UNITED STATES

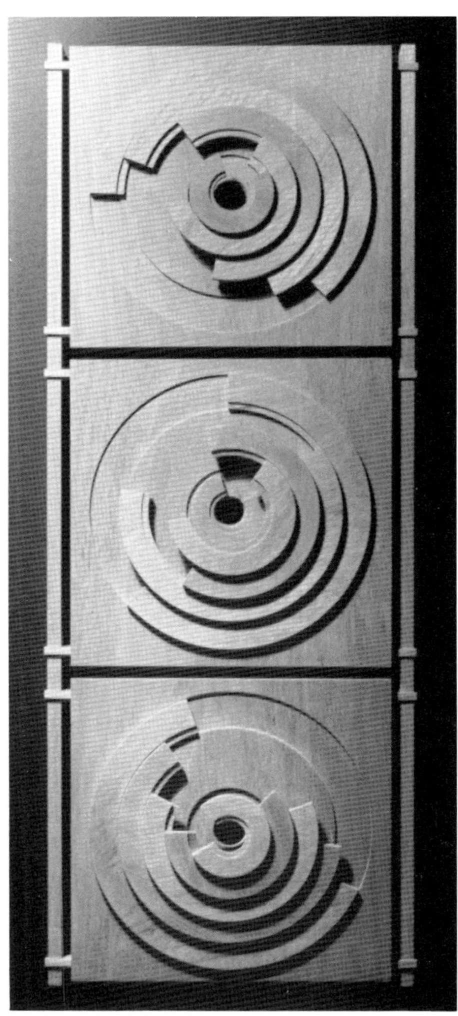

Wall Relief Sculpture. Honduras mahogany.
H. 22" x W. 10" x D. 3"

I work with a lot of *study pieces*, exploring various aspects of three-dimensional design and composition as it relates to turned forms. This particular work focuses upon curved linear and spacial relationships, profiled in relief form.

CHRISTOPHER WEILAND
PENNSYLVANIA, UNITED STATES

Chapter Eight:

FURNITURE

The challenge with *Walking Stool* was to create an animated piece with lathe derived components. The antique shoemaker "lasts" that were used as feet were amidst the rubbish in my studio that once housed a shoe factory. These feet inspired the trompe l'oeil seat and suede trim.

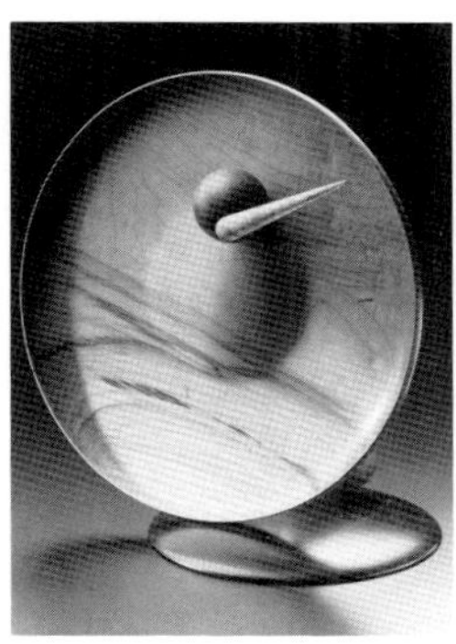

NEIL J. DONOVAN
PENNSYLVANIA, UNITED STATES

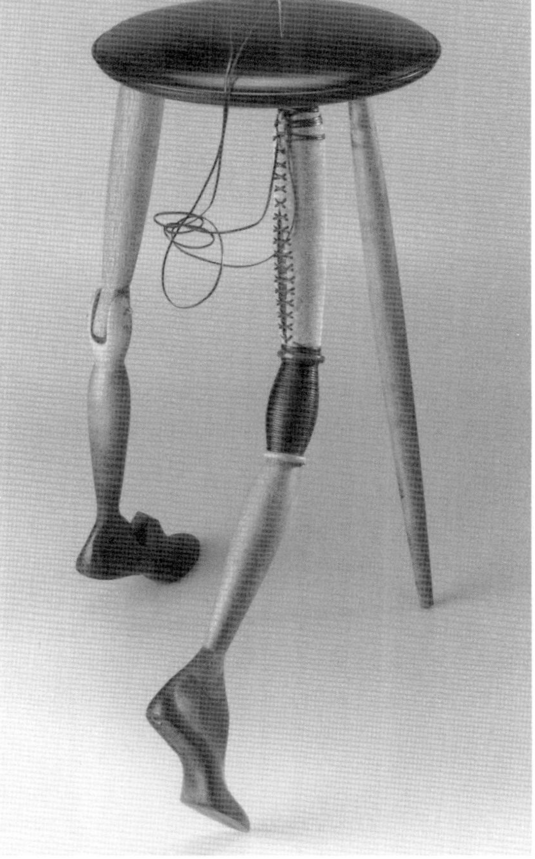

Walking Stool. Mahogany, oak, maple, suede, leather lace, antique shoemaker lasts. H. 28" x Diam. 12"

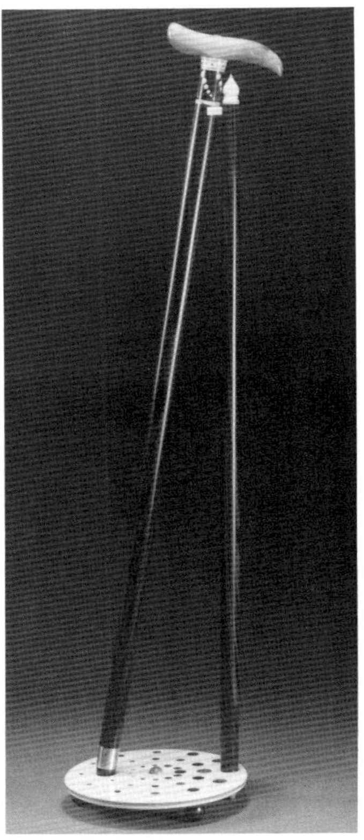

Cane on Stand. Ebony, pink ivory-wood, rosewood, bone, Corian. H. 33" x Diam. 7 1/2"

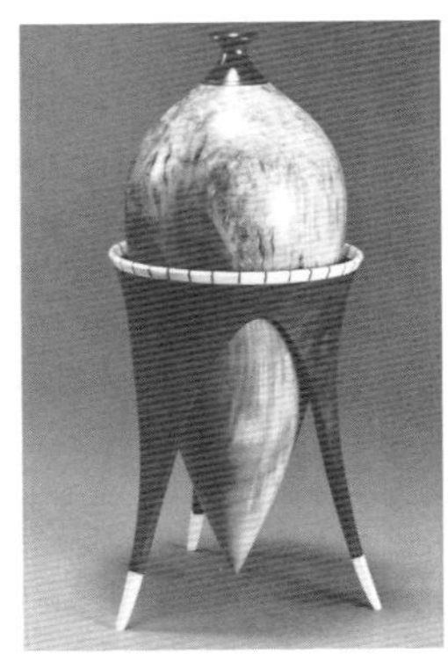

We have a very dear friend who is 85 years old. In 1988, my wife and I accompanied him on a tour to the Copper Canyon area of Mexico. On one of our stops I picked up an old weathered stick of some unidentified wood. I smoothed off the top and presented it to our friend as a walking aid. He has used it ever since.

I felt our friend deserved something better, so I set out to design and fabricate a cane that he would truly be proud to use. After completing the cane I was challenged to make a stand to display it on when not in use. The material I chose to use for the cane and stand were pink ivory for the handle and inlays; Macassar ebony for the staff, vertical support and feet of the stand; Brazilian rosewood for inlays; bone for the plug on the handle; Corian (an acrylic plastic) for the stand base, support tip, and cane inlays; and a bronze ferrule and rubber tip on the bottom end of the cane.

Designing and fabricating these pieces was quite different from anything I had tried before, but the challenge was exciting and quite rewarding for when I presented the cane and stand to our friend, he was somewhat overwhelmed.

P.S. I think, however, he will continue to use his old weathered stick and just look at his new one.

JACK ROGERS
ALABAMA, UNITED STATES

Captured Sphere. Wood, lacquer. H. 14" x W. 11" x D. 14"

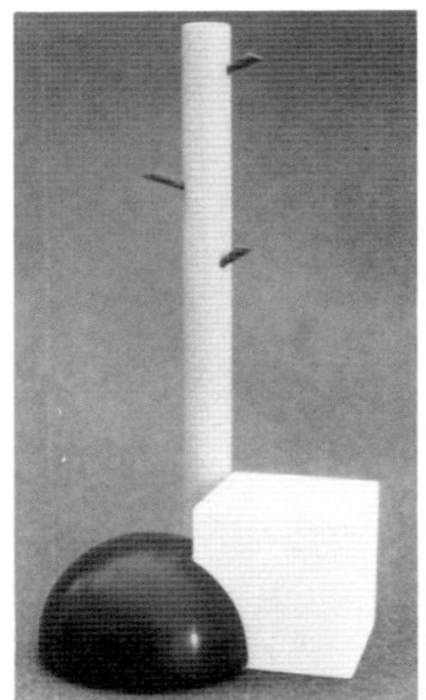

The concept was to achieve a well-balanced design, in this case a coat rack, whose elements were all lathe turned and not just lathe turned pieces added to a formal furniture form.

Concave (the square), convex (the sphere), and ordinary spindle turning (the spikes) were employed.

MICHAEL N. GRAHAM
CALIFORNIA, UNITED STATES

This piece represents my first exploration of vessel forms in furniture. The turned bowl/seat was derived from the image of a chair as a container for the body. Integrating this seat with the necessary structure of the chair and with the historical references provided a design and technical challenge. The lathe proved to be an effective tool for shaping volumetric parts and will undoubtedly be useful in the future for more than turned legs.

DOUG JONES
CONNECTICUT, UNITED STATES

Vanity Chair. Bleached white oak, upholstery.
H. 34" x W. 20" x D. 24"

This piece was developed and designed in collaboration with Veena Singh from Sansar Gallery in Washington, DC. Emphasis was obviously placed upon turned components both structurally and visually. The delicacy of fitted hinge members and lightly scored surface treatments accentuate objects displayed within.

CHRISTOPHER WEILAND
PENNSYLVANIA, UNITED STATES

[See photo of earlier work on page 44.]

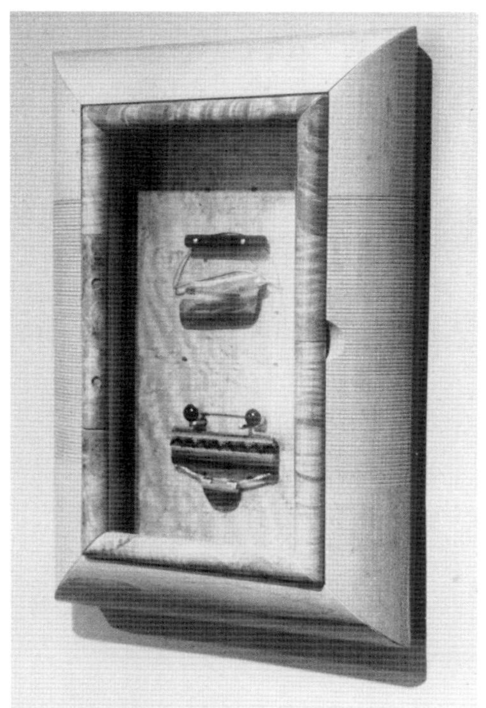

Display Jewelry Box. Maple, glass.
H. 14" x W. 10" x D. 3"

Vanity Table. The application of a spindle turned leg conjures up certain types of imagery. These legs appear anything but turned. The overall turned form is the same for each leg but the cutting and carving gives each leg its own character. Each leg is structural but also precarious.

Chatter Table. The painted legs help accentuate the form of the *chatter* turnings.

Vanity Table. Wenge, bubinga, maple. H. 29" x W. 38" x D. 18"

Chatter Table. Fountain head, white oak, milk paint. H. 34" x W. 48" x D. 15"

MARK SFIRRI
PENNSYLVANIA, UNITED STATES

Table. The leg placement grew out of the design for the shape of the top. (See comments for *Vanity Table.*) The paint and gold leaf add highlight to the form.

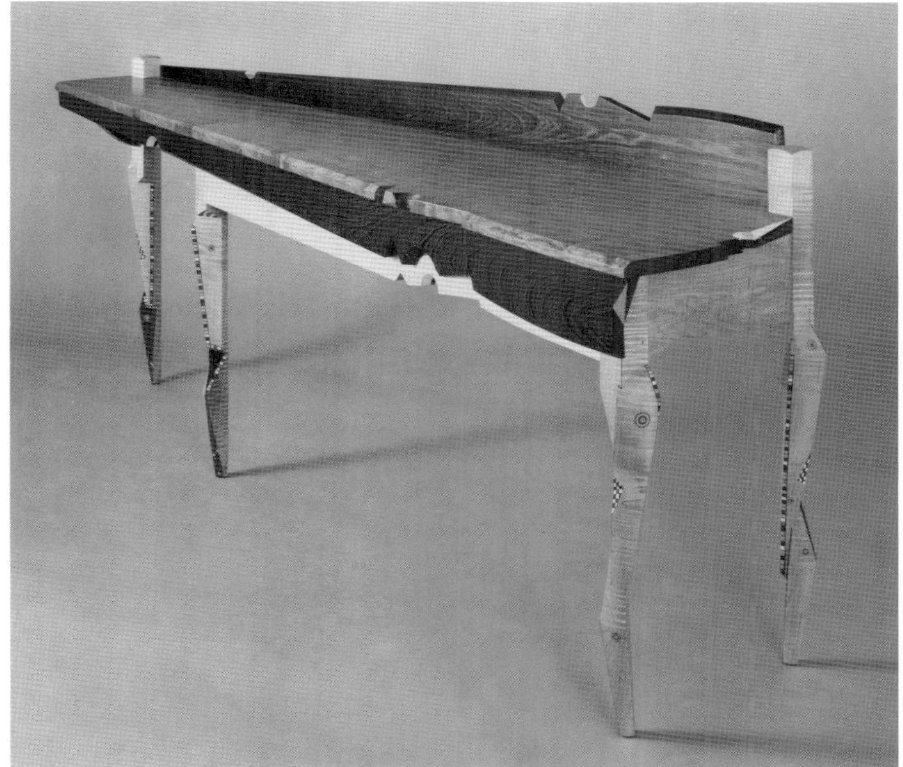

Table. Bubinga, wenge, maple, acrylic, gold leaf. H. 30" x W. 80" x D. 18"

MARK SFIRRI AND ROBERT DODGE
PENNSYLVANIA, UNITED STATES

I have wanted to make a chess set for a long time. About a year ago, I had made a series of turned miniature covered vessels. I received many comments from colleagues and customers that they looked like chess pieces, so I figured, what the Hell!

I had the crafts show at the Armory coming up, so I decided to make a chess set and chess table. I consulted with a chess grandmaster about the features he would like to have on an ultimate chess table, as well as dimensions and ideas about the pieces. I decided to make the pieces similar enough to the Staunton (standard) pieces so that a collector who also is a player would feel comfortable using them. The Knight, of course, was a departure, since I could not turn a horse, so it is a knight with a shield. The pieces are loosely representational to the characters they portray. The table and board are tournament standard proportions. The whole piece, *Chess Master*, was a labor of love.

Chess Master. Aluminum, Corian, leather, rubber, wood. H. 28" x W. 30" x W. 30"

PETER HANDLER
PENNSYLVANIA, UNITED STATES

Hats Off to Woodturning Series. Black cherry. H. 5" x Diam. 15"

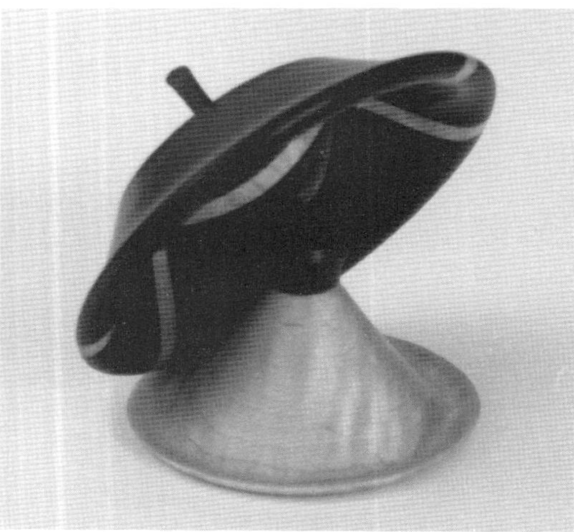

Box-Top. Ebony, curly maple, snakewood.
H. 4" x Diam. 6"

CHAPTER NINE:
OFF THE WALL

[See photo of earlier work on page 44.]

My inspiration to turn wood hats came from none other than Albert LeCoff. It was an idea I had in my head for some eight or nine years, but was not sure if it would work as I envisioned it.

Then last November (1990), at the occasion of Albert and Tina's "country western" wedding, I decided to give my idea a try. That first clumsy attempt was successful and well-received, so I pursued further hat turning. I have developed new techniques since then, to make the hats thinner, lighter and quite comfortable and wearable.

Since starting this I have become intensely aware of the many styles of hats. My hope and aspiration is to develop whatever techniques necessary to someday produce them all in wood.

With a thickness now of under 1/8" a finished hat only weighs nine ounces—no heavier than a *real* hat. I'm already cold bending fresh turned wet wood and getting as much as a 1" deflection in the brim when dry. Imagine one day with steam and or Downey maybe a *Tri-Cornered* or a *Ozzie* bush hat.

Second view: closed.

It seems to me that turned wood boxes are somewhat boring and should be able to do more than just contain something.

At Christmas time, while toying with some of each (boxes and tops) that I had made as gifts, my wife discovered that one item could be both. Needless to say I jumped on the idea. We now have a *vessel* that, if you place the top of the box on the table and the bottom of the box on it, add a finger spin, the bottom becomes the *top*. And will entertain—for five minutes per spin—anyone bored with simply a box.

JOHANNES MICHELSEN
VERMONT, UNITED STATES

I push each piece to be different from the previous work I have done.

With each turning I do I try and explore new avenues of approach. I use the lathe primarily as a design tool.

MICHAEL J. BROLLY
PENNSYLVANIA, UNITED STATES

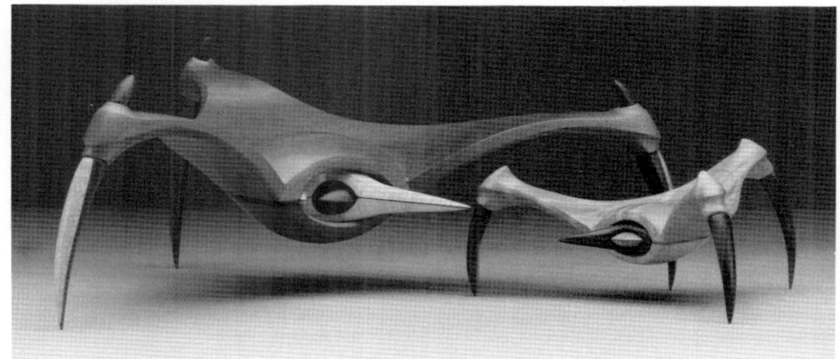

Mother/Daughter: Hunter/Prey II. Mahogany, maple, bubinga, purpleheart, ebony, dyed veneer. H. 6" x W. 14" x D. 14"

Frog Bowl II. Mahogany, maple, ebony, bubinga. H. 4" x W. 4" x D. 6"

It is very exciting for me to utilize my love of carving with my passion for turning. My current work combines turning techniques with sculptural concepts that have been evolving for me over the past twenty years. [In *Disc Series #4*] the two maple forms represent an exploration into lips. As these shapes evolved it seemed only appropriate to add the tongue.

RIC STANG
NEW JERSEY, UNITED STATES

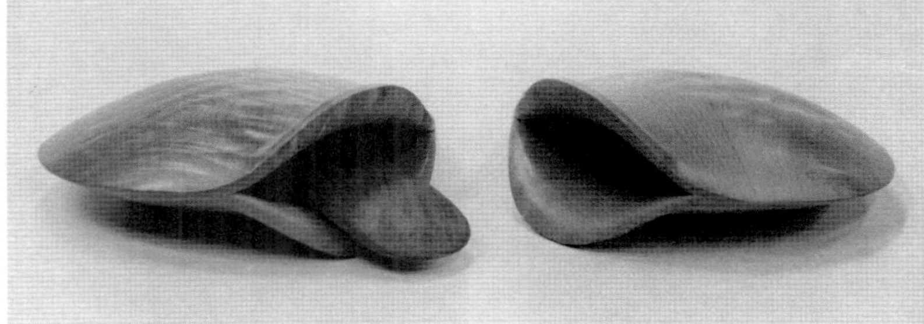

Disc Series #4. Curly maple. H. 8" x W. 8" x D. 4"

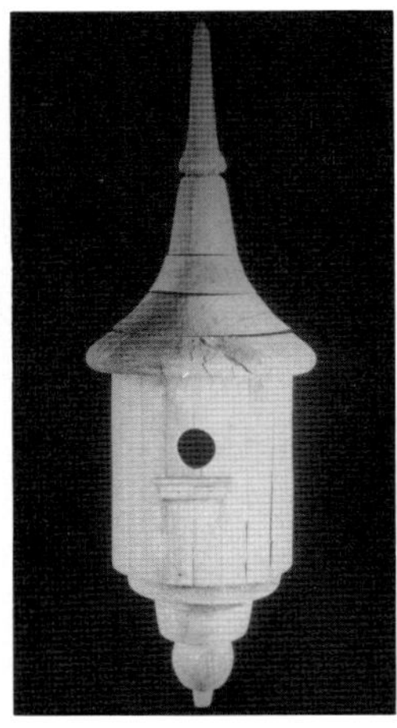

Aviary Abode. Scrap pine, cherry. H. 20"

Portrait of Wren Cottage. Ash.
H. 10" x Diam. 7"

Aviary Abode. My challenge has been to resist the temptation to make precious objects, and instead make use of humble materials to convey ideas which have value. In *Aviary Abode* I used scrap pine principally, and assembled it into an architectonic form with the intent of giving the impression of a "classic form". (Although there is no precedent for a classic turned birdhouse form.) *Aviary Abode* was made in 1991 as the subject of an article for *Woodturning* magazine, issue #3. Part of my ongoing challenge is to communicate, and stimulate, thought in others by writing about my work.

Portrait of Wren Cottage in Ash. The wood for this project was from a dead ash tree fallen in my backyard. My challenge was to communicate the notion that the life of a tree may end but the tree is still actively sustaining life. I was challenged to create a form which was aesthetic but did not distract from the message that the cycle continues. Life goes on, as evidenced by the textured surface of the wood. Even a dead tree provides a home and food for birds.

ANDREW LAW BARNUM
NEW YORK, UNITED STATES

PART THREE

CONTEXT

CHAPTER TEN:

NARRATIVE

A fun piece with a minimal approach—turned, lacquered, assembled—a statement of trees and the careful management of our forests.

GLENN ELVIG
MINNESOTA, UNITED STATES

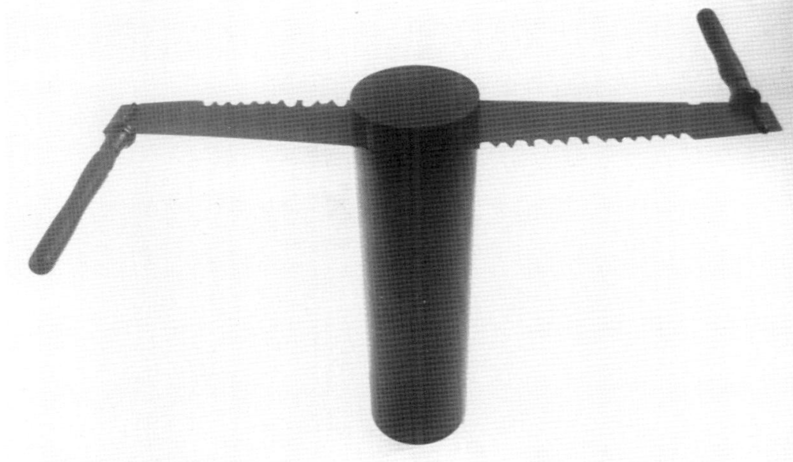

Wait A Minute Dad. Lacquered mahogany, steel saw. H. 36" x W. 20" x D. 56"

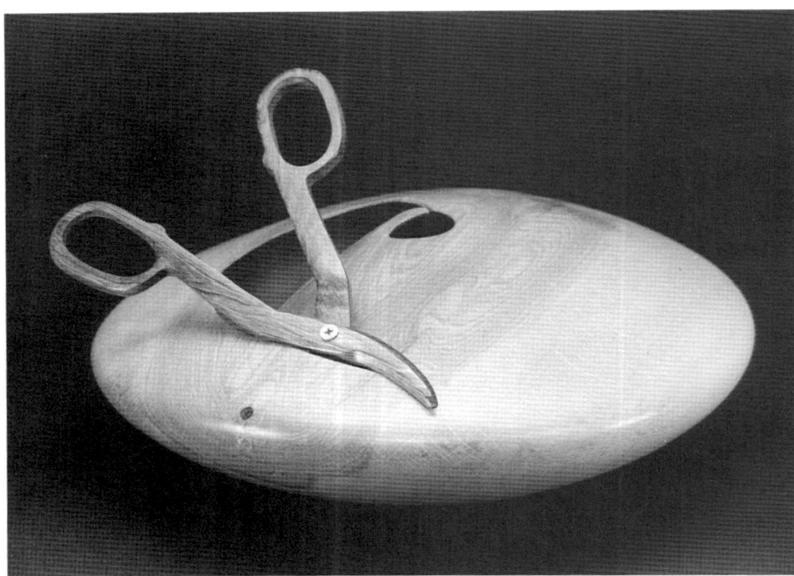

Curious. Beech, cocobola. H. 7" x Diam. 16"

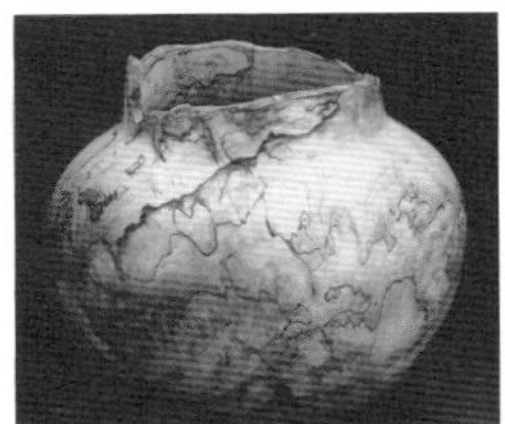

Primarily using the whole range of wood turning techniques I seek to maximize the inherent beauty of an individual piece of wood through a singular shape. Except in some constructions it is a subtractive experience. Sometimes drawing on traditional and classic forms, other times seeking a more immediate contemporary form.

Curiouss . . . an often asked-about technique . . . so on whimsey I decided to show them.

DAVID WENTZ
WEST VIRGINIA, UNITED STATES

Nest Goblet. Oak and hickory.
H. 10" x Diam. 6 1/2"

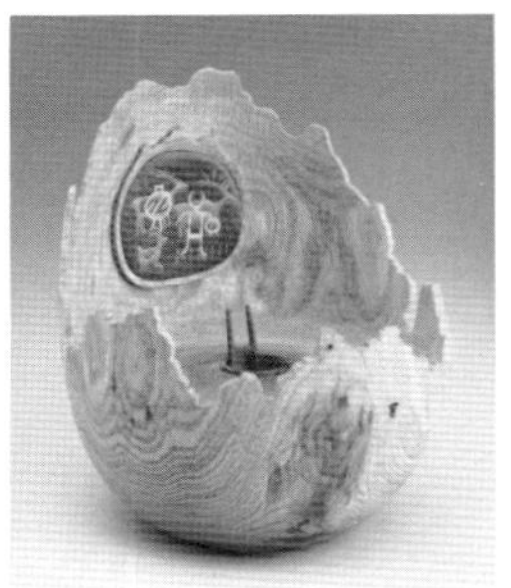

Nest Goblet. The challenge in this piece was to turn a goblet that was thin at the top and then gradually and evenly got thicker so that when I cut through to make the branches they have the correct visual *weight* to them. Because I am cutting away much of the wood, all of the way from the top to the bottom, any variations in wall thickness are very visible. The tiny egg that opens was a bit of a trick too.

TOM RAUSCHKE
WISCONSIN, UNITED STATES

Maturus is Latin for ripe. *Maturus* is one in a series of sculptural containers I made as a reflection on some intense personal feelings . . . *Maturus* is about aging.

The external physical appearance and interior reality do not always correspond. The ripe decaying form contains the growing seed. Decay starts from within, where it can evolve dramatically, but the drama is often not visible on the outside.

Maturus investigates the internal and external transformation caused by the ripening of experience and the experience of ripening.

STEPHEN HOGBIN
ONTARIO, CANADA

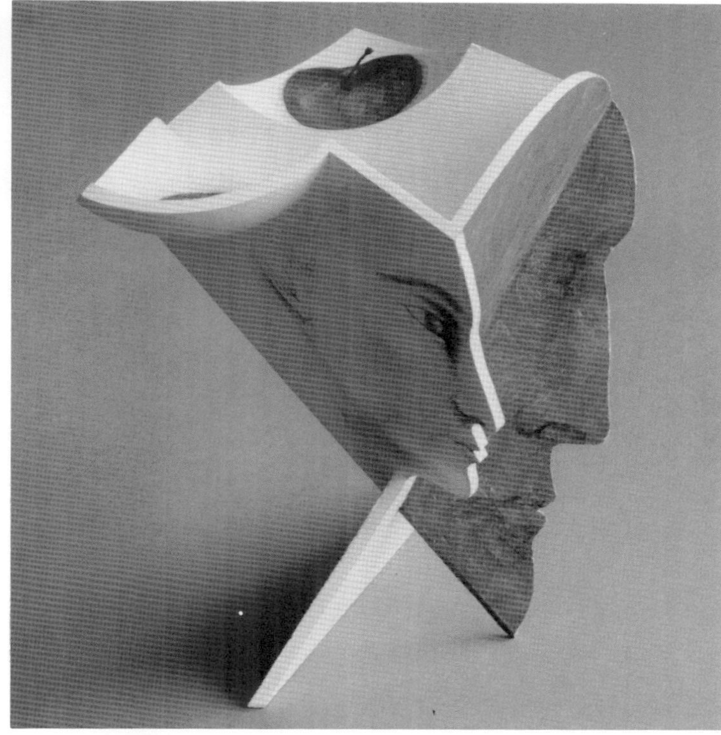

Maturus. Wood, paint, pencil. H. 9 1/2" x W. 9" x D. 8"

Chalice for a Corn Palace is an extension of my exploration of vegetable forms applied as sculptural and structural elements to "utilitarian" objects. The *Chalice* is turned and carved, and as a departure from many of my "Vege Tables" and "Flying Vegetables" utilizes the natural color of the wood (pau amarella, maple, and poplar) rather than using painted surfaces to reinforce the vegetable forms.

The double-walled construction is a return to a technique I developed and explored briefly circa 1982.

CRAIG NUTT
ALABAMA, UNITED STATES

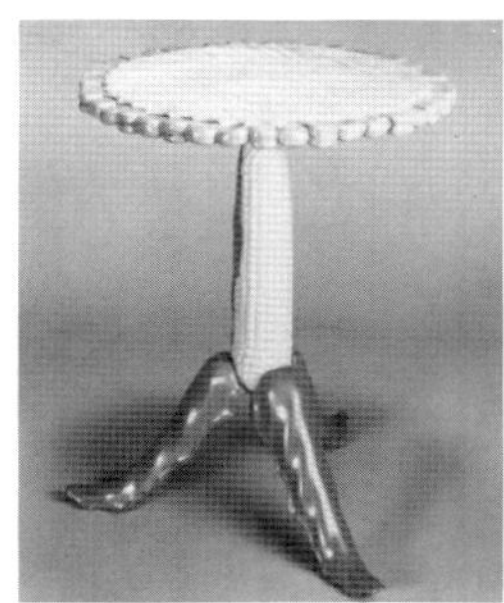

Chalice for a Corn Palace. Pau amarella, curly maple, poplar. H. 7" x Diam. 4 3/8"

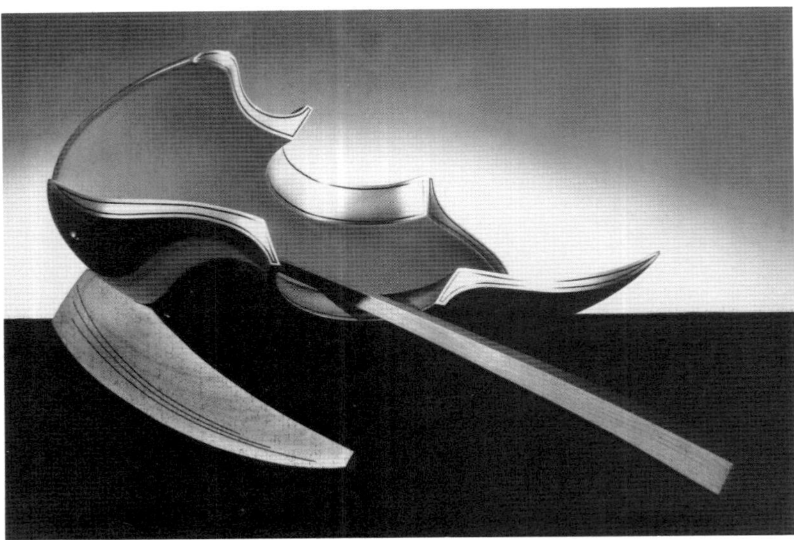

Relationships III, Startruck The Movie . . . in Which the Spaceship is Cleverly Disguised as a Pita Sandwich. Lacquered mahogany, cherry, brass.
H. 18" x W. 24" x D. 24"

[See photo of earlier work on page 34.]

This piece began as a collaboration between a group of students from University of Pennsylvania, Chris Weiland and myself. The idea was to turn a 24" platter, then make it *not a platter*, but finish with a strong sculpture. This was accomplished in three sessions: the first was a weekend at I.U.P. in October 1989, the second was three days at my studio in August 1990, and I finished the piece in October 1990 for the symposium at Arrowmont School.

The decisions on what the platter would become took a lot of time and were reached in an interesting manner: the group chose a moment when I was discussing other business with a client, looked at the various objects and photographs I have around, coupled these with what they already knew about me and my work, and cut the parts. From there we refined the parts until we ran out of time. Later I finished the parts, applied the colors, and assembled the piece. The complete title finally came to me in 1991.

GILES GILSON
NEW YORK, UNITED STATES

NIHIL SUB SOLE NOVUM . . .

MICHAEL N. GRAHAM
CALIFORNIA, UNITED STATES

Je L'ai Vue, Dans Une Revue.
Wood, lacquer, Corian.
H. 18" x W. 6" x D. 6"

CHAPTER ELEVEN:
RITUAL AND FETISH

Future Species was turned, carved, painted, then carved again to get the texture.

I have included the piece [photo] previous to this one, but more significant is the one that came after, *Self-Portrait—Introvert.* The only turned process was the form it was made on. I made it after *Future Species* which were time-consuming and picky. I grabbed whatever materials were in the shop and finished it in one day. I just had to make something that was fast.

We are all in this together.

MICHAEL HOSALUK
SASKATCHEWAN, CANADA

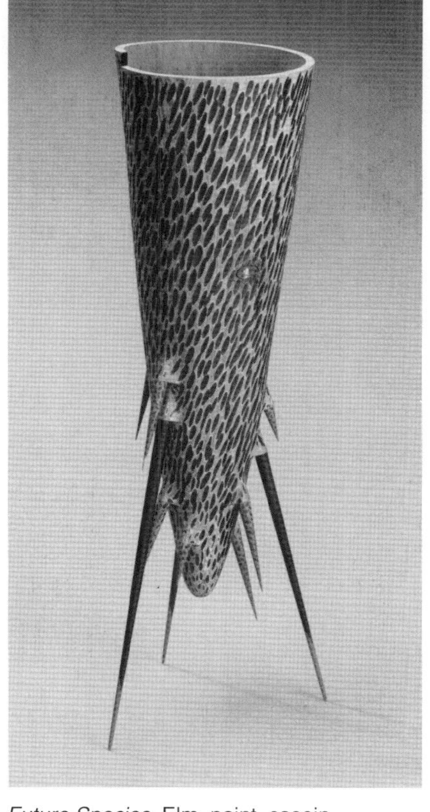

Future Species. Elm, paint, casein.
H. 12" x Diam. 4"

Untitled. Wood and brass. H. 17" x W. 4" x L. 36"

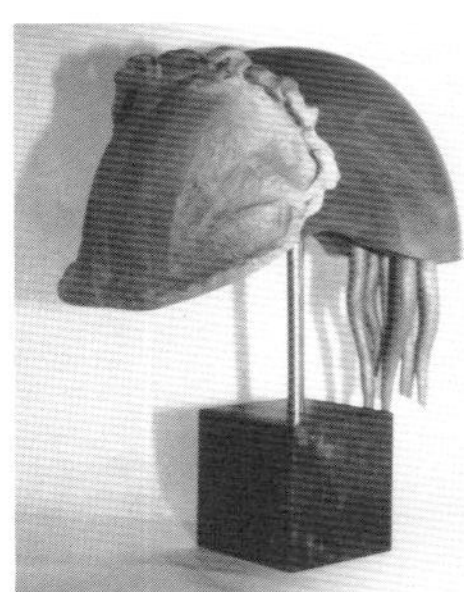

The Challenge. The turning point for me was in changing my attitude towards the uses of the lathe. Previously, I had seen it used primarily as a tool for making bowls and candlesticks.

The Challenge was to use the lathe to fashion a much larger piece of work. Something much more intricate and liberating. This ship is the result.

Presently I am exploring many directions using the lathe as the main tool of design.

LOUIS ALVAREZ
ONTARIO, CANADA

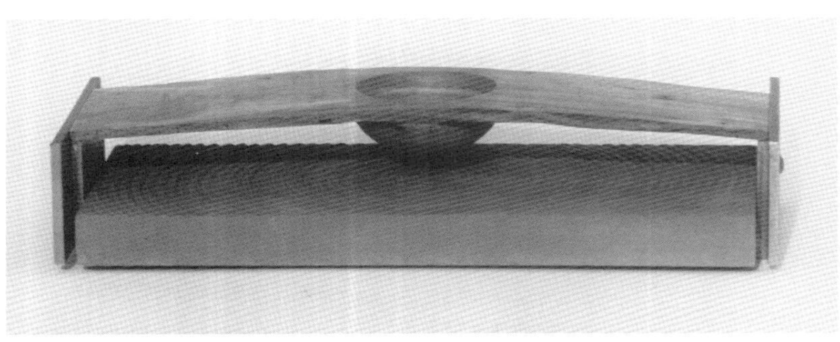

Bridge Bowl. Soft maple, beech, steel. H. 3 1/2" x W. 17 1/2" x D. 7 1/2"

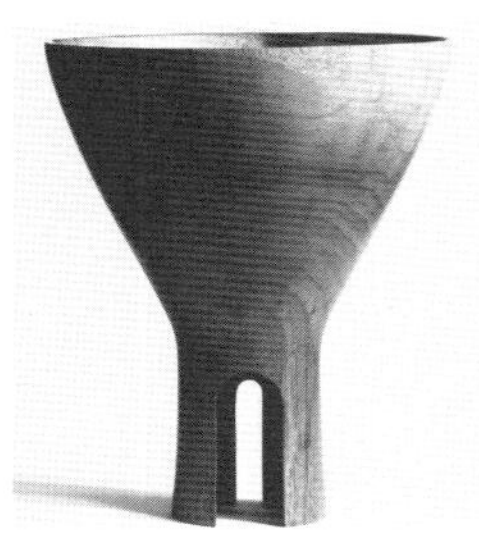

The challenge of *Bridge Bowl* was in the use of color. The simple, obvious, sky blue water color was such a departure from the natural wood, plain steel, stone and matte black surfaces I ordinarily use, that I felt as if I had dangled a toe off the edge of the world; and, dream-like, created a new bit of world to stand on.

Just a little step really, but such a pleasure. I like it.

DON KELLY
MASSACHUSETTS, UNITED STATES

TRI-18,000. Genuine mahogany, purpleheart, aluminum.
H. 6 1/2" x W. 7 1/2" x D. 6 1/4"

TRI-18,000 is the latest in a series of forms which investigate triaxial form in space. It consists of three dominant forms which are juxtaposed to create a relational triad. Collectively they and other elements interact to form numerous spatial relationships.

MICHAEL CHINN
IOWA, UNITED STATES

The impetus for these works grew out of another interest of mine: the making and playing of Djembés, an African percussion instrument. In the fall of 1990 I stopped making sculptural work, turning instead 15 drum bodies. Djembés are traditionally hacked out with chisels and hatchets which gives them an organic unsymmetrical form, a feeling I tried to retain by moving away from my usual refined surfaces to unsanded, textured ones, not fussing over line, applying free hand patterns, etc.

As I worked I reflected on the paucity of American tribal objects; that is, objects locally made of readily available materials each one similar but individual and closely connected to the life of the owner. There are Americans making tribal objects—the Hopi or Vietnamese immigrant—but these objects are Hopi or Vietnamese, not specifically "American."

So, I undertook to make the objects I would want an archeologist to find—remarkably preserved—in a cave 1500 years from now. Objects of mysterious purpose, that had been used, cared for, were of some significance to their owners.

Meanwhile, back here in the past, a design revolution was going in my head and a number of significant idea/perceptions took place. For example, the introduction of lacing left me with a number of string ends to deal with. While mulling this over, I noticed that the long trailing ends grounded the piece, fairing it into the universe. So I left them. These pieces should be displayed with the string—out and integrated with their surroundings. In this way the piece has a constant potential for change, can be participated in, is different in different places. It is alive and connected to the world.

RICHARD GILLAM
MAINE, UNITED STATES

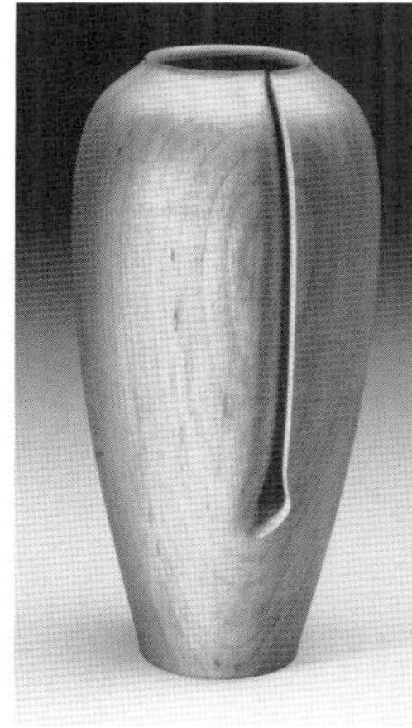

American Tribal Artifact #1. Wood, rope.
H. 12 1/4" x Diam. 8 3/4"

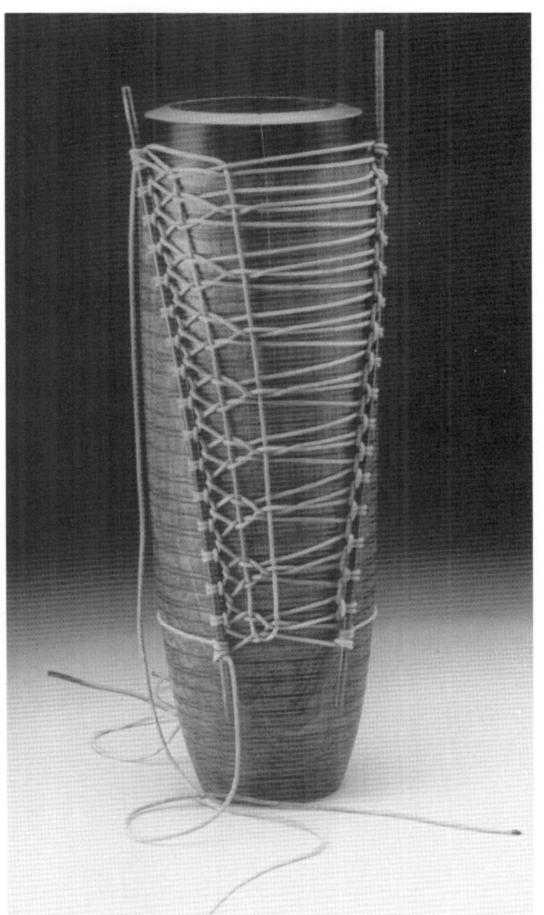

American Tribal Artifact #3. Wood, rope, bronze rod.
H. 20" x Diam. 7 3/4"

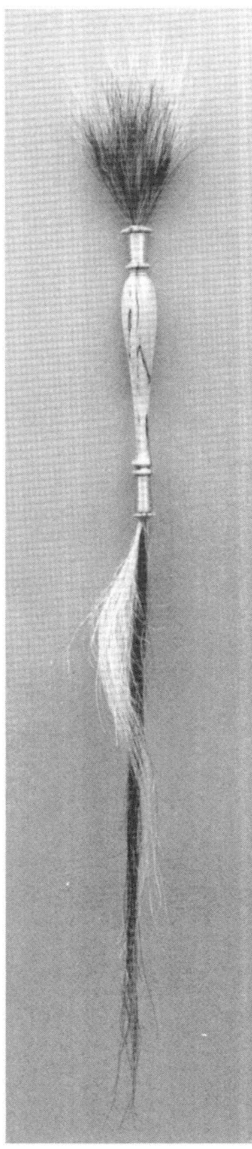

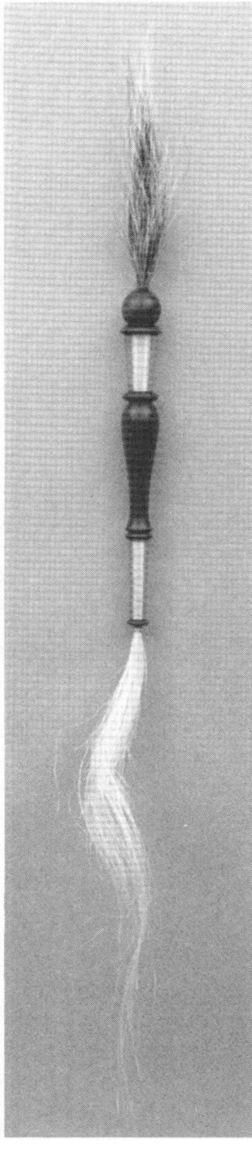

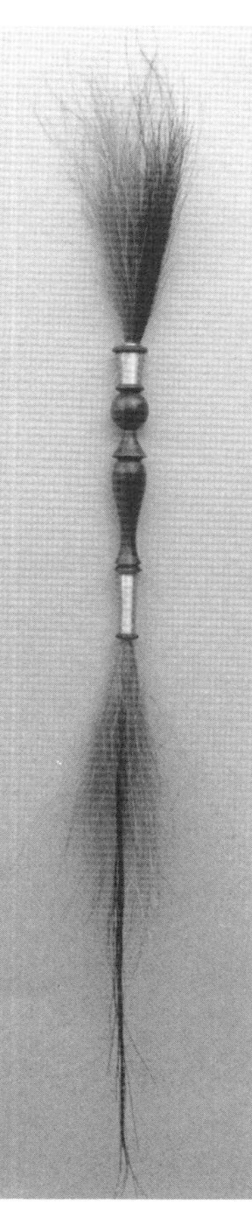

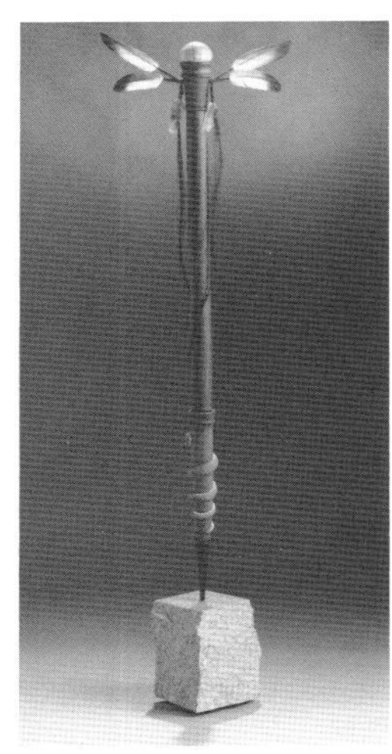

Whispering Spirit #1.
Spalted maple, horse
hair, squirrel hair,
gold wire.
H. 10" x Diam. 3/8"

Whispering Spirit #2.
Macassar ebony,
horse hair, squirrel
hair, gold wire.
H. 10" x Diam. 3/8"

Whispering Spirit #3.
Macassar ebony,
horse hair, copper
wire.
H. 10" x Diam. 3/8"

Whispering Spirit Series. In order to express the ideas set forth in this series, I found it necessary to work on a very small scale using very delicate materials. As a challenging technical exercise, it was a little like trying to tie your shoes with a spider web, or attempting to put a bra on a flea - often frustrating, and not always successful the first time through.

The origin of the *Whispering Spirit* is a mystery to me. As Georgia O'Keefe said: "I paint things that I don't know about". . . there is an element of the unknown, like the profound thought that appears lucid in a dream, only to evaporate with the waking day. The real challenge for me is to capture that fleeting thought, to freeze it in space, to solidify the ethereal into something that can be held—ever so delicately —in hopes that it may speak softly to you the secret that vanished with your dreams.

MARK J. BURHANS
OHIO, UNITED STATES

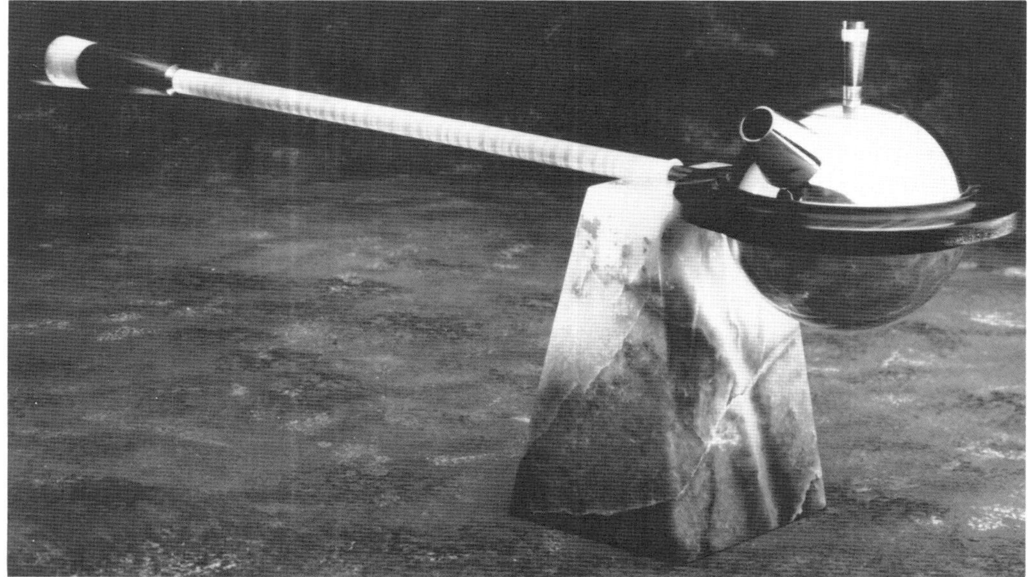

Tea Balance. Brass, ebony, maple, soapstone. H. 9" x W. 24" x D. 5 1/2"

[See earlier photo and statement on page 29.]

WILLIAM MOORE
OREGON, UNITED STATES

The *Tightwire* series is a study of balance and form. It has a long vertical component with motion starting at the tiny ebony foot, moving up the ever-widening column and finally opening out at the top into a slightly flattened, slightly flared rim of ebony.

. . . earlier attempts had appendages protruding from their sides in tripod form or large base components. Neither approach proved satisfactory. The accompanying photo depicts one of the first attempts at piercing the vessel with [brass] rod forms.

. . . I soon switched from brass rods to silver tubing that has a hardened steel shaft in the center for rigidity. It soon became evident that the tension produced as the two rods nearly meet above the rim of the vessel became the crucial signature to the work.

BUD LATVEN
NEW MEXICO, UNITED STATES

Tightwire N. 24. Cristobol, ebony, silver, veneers. H. 12 1/2" x W. 8 1/2" x D. 7"

Pierced Geode 407 is in the *Pierced Geode* Series. The face on the *geode* deals with centers and the contrasting lines of the two sliding dovetails. The hole, the routed groove and the outside shape are on three different centers, stressing the cylindrical base of turning, then pierced through with the linear dark dovetails.

There is a more sculptural feeling to *Maple Geode 420* dealing with contrast in four degrees: natural burl surface, chainsaw-carved surface, smooth maple, and gold leafed maple, laid inside leaf-shaped folds.

ROBYN HORN
ARKANSAS, UNITED STATES

Pierced Geode 407. Maple burl, Madagascar rosewood. H. 13" x W. 16" x D. 12"

Maple Geode 420. Western maple burl, gold leaf. H. 15 1/2" x W. 14 1/2" x D. 15 1/2"

CHAPTER TWELVE:
TOTEMIC

T47N, R22W. Birch.
H. 48" x Diam. 10"

The basis of the form is "organic" in nature, in that it is derived through the manipulation of whole logs in such a way that parts of the natural surface are left intact, and the forms and hues follow the activity of the layers of the wood. All of these works contain parts with similar concave/convex surfaces which are attached to one another in such a way which exhibits a corresponding directionality of concave/convex members within each piece. My first experience with this idea in the form of a wooden object followed the completion of a commission for nine "natural edge" salad bowls, which were simply stacked.

The challenge in this series was to arrange the parts into an "organically symmetric" pattern whereby the high sides of each part are exposed over the low sides of the one beneath. Each of the works in this series features an assemblage of concave/convex shapes which create the visual sensation of intersecting arcs along the surface of the organically derived cambium edges.

The base portions were formed from the same wood as the upper parts and exhibit a continuity of hue and grain pattern. The intent was to create bases that would support the idea of the upper portions having grown out of them. This was accomplished by forming the wood in a way that the figure is changed by gradually turning the bark off the log so the upper portion of the base is similar in color and brightness to the "budding" section at the top of the work. The transition between the top of the bases and the bottom of the "buds" are converging arcs of the same degree.

T47N, R22W is the regeneration of an organic presence once provided by a very dear tree which blew down during a period of great destruction. The bark curls are reminiscent of the gale forces that provided the material and motivation to complete this piece.

E. RICK HARTOM
ILLINOIS, UNITED STATES

Capital-Lie-Zation is the largest and most complex turning I've attempted to date. It took over a year to come to completion. This work is an exploration of both the bowl and columnar forms. Many traditional techniques were employed: stave construction, spindle turning, as well as face-plate work. Some less-than-traditional techniques were also employed: sandblasted fluting, bowl separation by pins, as well as painting.

This work is also a covered bowl, albeit five-foot in height. The size of it alone forces one to interact with it. The top dome reminded me of the capitol, hence the name.

ROGER L. BARNES
NEW YORK, UNITED STATES

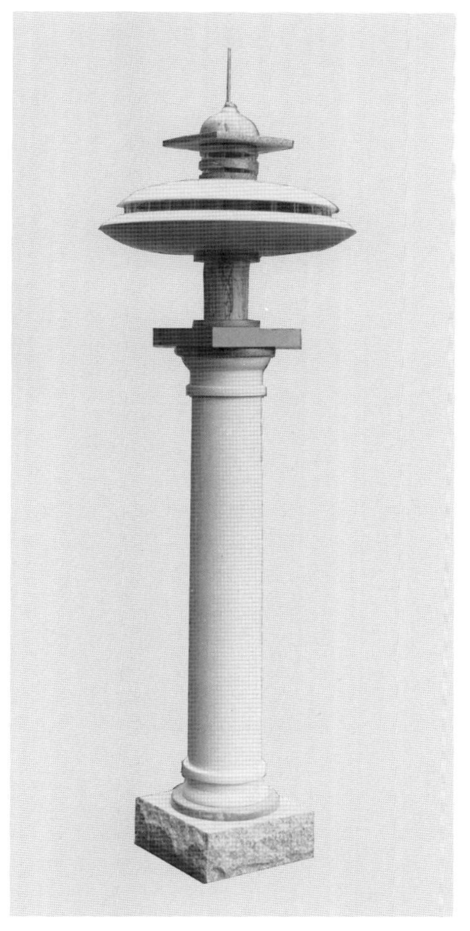

Capital-Lie-Zation. Maple, granite, avonite, acrylic. H. 60" x W. 17" x D. 17"

In *Migration* I attempted to give meaning to three similar turned forms . . . to evoke a sense of direction, movement and mystery.

[See photo of earlier work on page 36.]

CHRISTIAN BURCHARD
OREGON, UNITED STATES

Migration. Madrone burl, ash, black oak, dye. H. 31" x W. 13" x D. 5"

Redemption. Wood.
H. 52" x W. 24" x D. 19"

. . . As a sculptor my overall process is additive rather than subtractive . . . Here my intention was to create a more simple piece—a form which does include additive process and does become a construction, but does not require a more complex whole (in the physical sense) from which to draw its meaning. It seemed essential that the piece should look *made*, with no attempts to disguise joinery or signs of the mechanical process of turning; and yet equally essential, that it should suggest the possibility of having been evolved by nature. Consequently, in addition to the organic element of the branch, I prioritized any inherent tendencies in the material toward chaos . . . the pod-like form has split . . . to allow its essence to spill forth; meanwhile, the stem branches out, its extremities reaching toward the heavens.

. . . I find myself drawn to this pod/cone/top-like shape . . . the intention is to have it seem like something new each time; herein lies the primary aspect of challenge in this present work.

CHARLES FORSTER
OREGON, UNITED STATES

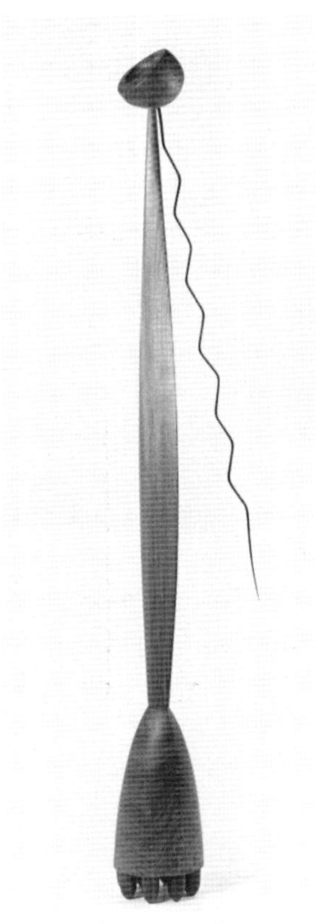

Silent Witness. Walnut,
ebonized oak.
H. 74" x W. 8" x D. 16"

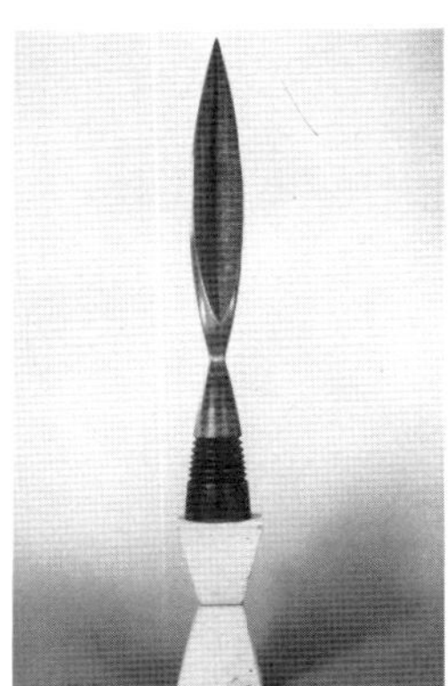

The work *Silent Witness* is an attempt to express the idea of a contented being moving from a subtle level of awareness into activity, as if awakening from a dream. Earlier work such as *The Receptive One* expresses a state of silent receptivity with no suggestion of a wakeful active state. In *Silent Witness* the asymmetrical body section, the zig-zag hair shape, and the multifooted base suggest a subtle stirring of activity. With *The Receptive One* the strict vertical symmetry and angular base imply no movement. Technically, *Silent Witness* includes offset turning, carving and bending. *The Receptive One* was turned on one axis and carved.

WILLIAM LEETE
MICHIGAN, UNITED STATES

I continue to departfrom the vessel format of my past. It started with the first *Turner's Challenge*, and the piece I entered of a peeling orb [shown]. From there, many variations of my *Winged Series* have emerged, exemplifying change and growth.

My latest pieces speak of balance and harmony between the feminine and masculine.

The delicate feminine wings support the masculine column, while the column grounds the lift of the wings. A vertical and horizontal balance exists between the two, with a sense of eternity from the ancientness of the cracking and burning.

TODD HOYER
ARIZONA, UNITED STATES

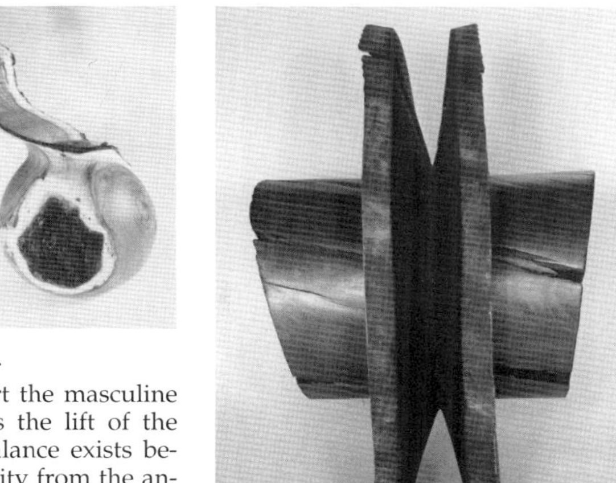

Winged Series, Suspended Column Variation, Eucalyptus.
H. 21" x W. 14" x D. 23"

This recent piece of work, *Columns and Vessels*, is a result of my desire to manipulate new and unchallenged materials and also my desire to express this material in a form consistent with previous studies. The underlying triadic structure of this work is based on the three totemic forms in my previous large piece, 'Anthropo-

morphics', which was made in 1988. In that work the attempt was to create a family of pieces without any particular cultural reference and yet have a distinctly anthropomorphic feel. Each totemic column in this piece consists of a two part structure, the lower column or body and the upper head or crown portion. The bare wood head form identifies the totem whereas the black body portion acts solely to give dimension and mass to the work.

In the current work the underlying allusion is also anthropomorphic but with an added architectural dimension. The mind can shift back and forth in its perception of these two dimensions while observing the work. Its architectural nature is evident in the choice of the obelisk-like columns which is enhanced by the cold surface of stainless steel. The horizontal texturing on the columns though, is unexpected in relation to its material surface. The upper portions of these columns are crowned with aluminum and copper-coated vessel forms which can act as either vessel-like head forms or upper segments to an architectural form depending on the choice of the perceiver.

BUD LATVEN
NEW MEXICO, UNITED STATES

Columns and Vessels. Metalized wood.
H. 90" x W. 36" x D. 24"

CHAPTER THIRTEEN:
POLITICAL

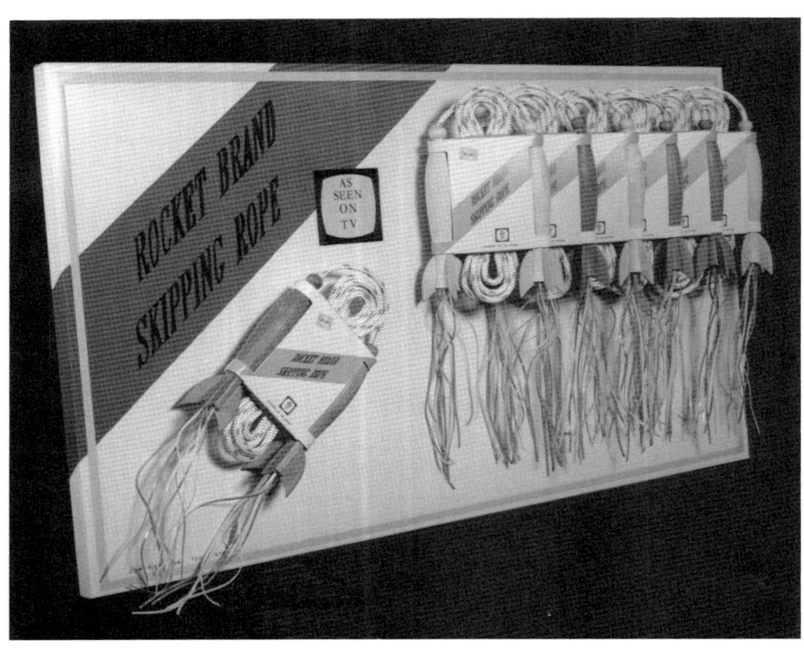

Our Children Watch. Mixed media. H. 17 1/4" x W. 30" x D. 4 1/2"

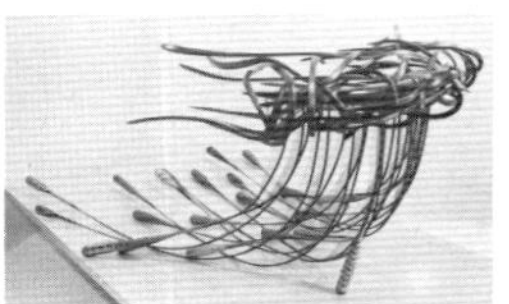

The idea for this piece, called *Our Children Watch,* came to me during the final days of the Gulf confrontation. My first image of this piece was of a smiling little girl, playfully skipping. In her hands was a beautiful skipping rope — the handles made of wood. This image at first seemed innocent and one that I could file away with all the rest but, as I focused harder on her twirling hands, I discovered that the handles were in the shape of rockets.

My challenge was to make a sculpture that allowed the viewer an insight into to my original image.

TED HUNTER
ONTARIO, CANADA

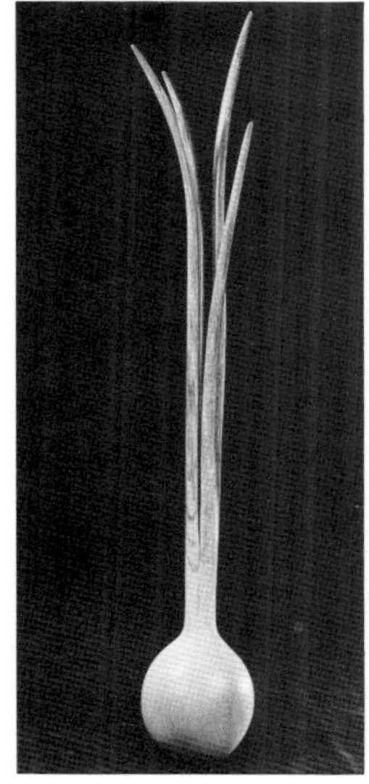

. . . Endangered Species [is one in] a group of sculptures executed to depict my apprehension about the state and future of the natural environment. In this body of new work, metaphysical concerns take precedent over utilitarian ones. The processes used in the creation of these works reflect nature's own way of sculpting.

Sandblasting was employed to create surface texture and fire because of its spiritual and mystical qualities. The forms resulting from these methods—like nature—have a spherical sense with no beginning and no end.

DAVID N. EBNER
NEW YORK, UNITED STATES

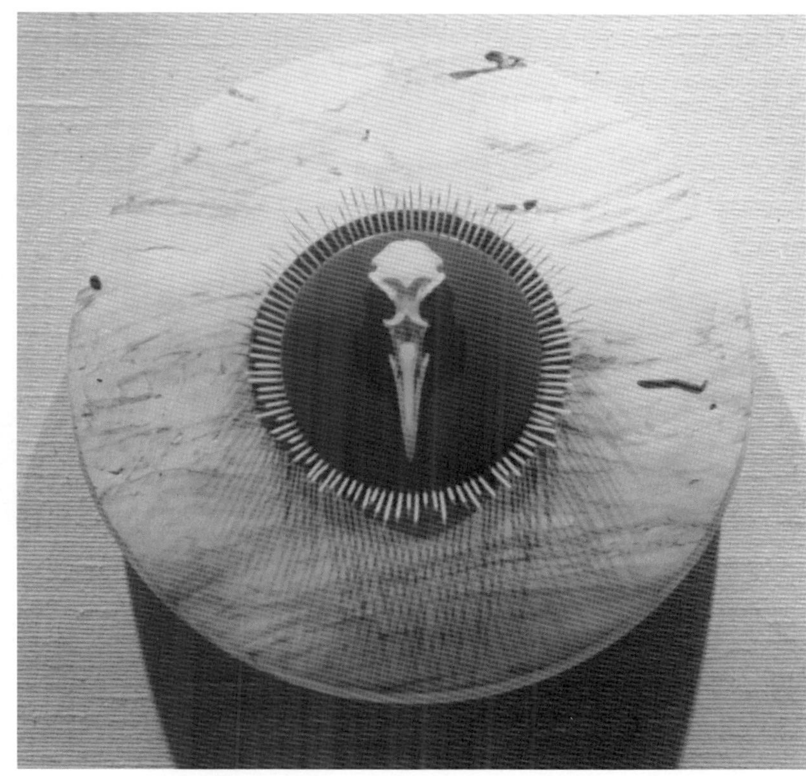

Endangered Species. Spalted beech, gull skull, porcupine quills. D. 4" x Diam. 16"

War Bowl is the first bowl I have made where I do not want to express beauty of some kind. The Gulf War, which is just over as I write this, has stirred up a lot of pain and confusion for me. I made this bowl to express some of these feelings. War destroys not only people and property, it also wounds the spirit.

Bowls can be seen as symbols of wholeness. My goal has always been to make bowls that radiate a sense of peace. This is a wounded bowl. It radiates disturbance.

[See photo of earlier work on page 8.]

ALAN STIRT
VERMONT, UNITED STATES

War Bowl. Ceanothus burl. H. 5 3/4" x Diam. 9"